A View from the Floor

Hugh B. Black

New Wine Press

New Wine Press
PO Box 17
Chichester PO20 6YB
England

ISBN: 1 874367 64 7

Other books by Hugh Black

The Baptism in the Spirit and Its Effects
Reflections on the Gifts of the Spirit
Reflections on a Song of Love (1 Corinthians 13)
A Trumpet Call to Women
The Clash of Tongues: With Glimpses of Revival
Consider Him (Twelve Qualities of Christ)
Battle for the Body
The Incomparable Christ
Gospel Vignettes
Reflections from Abraham
Reflections from Moses: With the Testimony of Daniel McVicar
Christ the Deliverer
Christian Fundamentals
Reflections from David
Pioneers of the Spiritual Way
Revival: Including the Prophetic Vision of Jean Darnall
Revival: Personal Encounters
Revival: Living in the Realities
War in Heaven and Earth
E.H. Taylor: A Modern Christian Mystic (edited by Hugh Black)

Typeset by CRB Associates, Reepham, Norfolk
Printed in England by Clays Ltd, St Ives plc.

Dedication

To those who have recently met God
on His operating table

Contents

	Foreword *Alison Speirs*		7
	Preface		9
Chapter 1	**The Coming of Blessing** Jennifer O – Ishbel – Alan – Anne – Julia – Isa		11
Chapter 2	**From Glory to Glory** Elaine – Tony – Diana – Janet		27
Chapter 3	**The Coming of Song:** **A Wind from Lindisfarne** Sarah		39
Chapter 4	**Healing Power** Margaret M – Comfort – Mike		47
Chapter 5	**To Work, to War** Isobel – Eric		63
Chapter 6	**Cleaning the Tiles** Andrew – Margaret Y – Pat		73
Chapter 7	**Within the Veil** Irene		85
Chapter 8	**To Fall or Not to Fall** Pauline – Susie – Anita – Alison		91
Chapter 9	**A Rich Foreshadowing** Jennifer J – Diana – Mary		107

5

Foreword

I have known Hugh Black and been a member of Struthers Memorial Church for ten years, during which time the teaching, ministry and example have led me into a deep love for Christ and completely changed my life.

It was my privilege to be present during the early days of what we called 'the new ministry' and to be a witness to the life-changing effects of it on many people personally known to me.

I remember well the meetings, the expectancy, the effects; but more, with the anointing to minister, came an awesome presence of the Living God which at once had a magnetizing effect on the heart and spirit and at the same time brought a conviction of the imperfect condition in which most of us live. This presence caused us to offer deep and heartfelt praise to God for the covering of the blood of His Son which alone allowed us to bear the weight of His glory.

I commend this book to you for the testimonies of many ordinary people who have had an encounter with God. These testimonies strengthen our faith and confidence in God's love towards us. I commend it more particularly for the sense of God which permeates its pages and brings an awe of the Holy One of Israel to our hungry souls.

Alison Speirs

Preface

There is a united service of the Struthers Memorial fellowship held regularly in Scotland on Saturday nights, and for many years these and certain other services have been taped. As a result a fairly accurate record of particular movements and trends can be traced.

Late in 1994 God began to move in a new way, and many people have testified to what He has done in their lives. In reading over some of the accounts I felt that there was much in them to encourage others, were they to be edited for publication. Hence this present book, the first of a trilogy.

On Saturday 12 November 1994, what I will call the new ministry commenced at a conference at High Wycombe in the south of England. It came suddenly and unexpectedly, although with hindsight I can see that certain events probably led up to it. I was amazed at the new incoming of God and the effects of His presence and power.

On the Saturday night following I was back in Scotland and felt that I should let our regular fellowship know of what had happened in High Wycombe and hopefully have them enter into similar blessing. Many responded and the flow of life has continued ever since.

With the new ministry came a wave of new songs which have brought constant blessing. The words of three of these are included in this book.

In keeping with the 'Cana' principle, the reader may rest assured that the best wine has not been exhausted in the first volume of the trilogy!

I wish to thank those who have allowed me to use their testimonies and other spoken or written contributions. I am grateful to my wife Isobel and to Jennifer Jack and Pauline Anderson for their suggestions and proofreading labours. In particular, my daughter Dr Alison Black has taken from my shoulders much of the burden of reshaping the material for publication.

Chapter 1

The Coming of Blessing

'An *operating table*? Surely not!'

Jennifer, a mature Christian, knew all about operating tables from her experience as a hospital laboratory technician. They had, she thought, nothing in common with the new ministry of the Holy Spirit that had brought many in our fellowship prostrate to the floor:

> Admittedly I had been a bit taken aback when the 'view from the floor' began to be current in our church. But as a committed Christian, baptized in the Holy Spirit for about eighteen years, I could not deny that we were experiencing an unusual visitation from God. And so I had gone forward for prayer on a few occasions and while on the floor had sensed a lovely nearness of Christ; once I had felt my whole body covered by a canopy of light.
>
> After that I demurred at Mr Black's description of 'God's operating table', which, given my connection with the medical profession, sounded singularly unappealing: in deference to my reaction he sometimes used the term 'God's couch'!

Then something happened that completely changed her mind about the idea of a comforting sofa:

It began at our February conference in Aberfoyle, when I was touched by God and sensed something deeper than ever before. Keen to find out what God wanted of me, I went for prayer in Glasgow the following weekend and found myself on the floor again. On this occasion I felt very uncomfortable, not to say slightly annoyed – a reaction I had experienced before but done nothing about. Now, however, I realized that God was wanting to do something, though I didn't know what.

At this point Jennifer sought help from Grace Gault, who had prayed with her at Aberfoyle and was used deeply in ministry.[1] She describes what happened when they came before God.

At first I felt on familiar territory. 'O Lord,' I prayed inwardly, 'please don't leave me here.' Having hungered for God for some time, I wanted more. Just at that point Grace described this hunger and encouraged me to let it rise – which I did until it was a pain within. Then in an unforgettable moment of time there was the sensation of a plaster being ripped off an infected wound (you know how you are always told that if you rip it off quick it won't hurt), and underneath I saw a whole unresolved area of my childhood. Christ was seeking access to an area of my inner being to which I had admitted nobody. It was in fact where 'I' really was – the real me, not the person I had let others see. I was shocked to realize I was holding Christ out.

The problem had its roots in her early background:

I came from a broken home, at a time when divorce was less common than now. My mother had brought me up to the very best of her ability in circumstances of great difficulty. From her I learned that life was tough but that you always got on with it. My only memory of my father, who had left when I was about seven, was an intense desire to see him and have him back. My most vivid impression was of his never turning up. My brother and I would wait at the window on a day he was supposed to take us out: sometimes he came, but more often he did not appear. I pushed this pain far down and covered it over. I always imagined he would return – and even after he was dead the effect had not died with him. Put simply, I had kept a part of my heart for him, even though it could never be, and therefore my heart did not all belong to God.

I was stunned, and during the following week, although I had felt Christ actually walking into this part, I also felt Him probing out the pain. Grace prayed with me the next Saturday, as the wound had been opened but not healed. I showed all the pain to Christ and sobbed as I had never done before. (I had always liked to think I was in control of my feelings, but God was doing a work that I did not want to hinder.) I remember especially telling Christ about being left, and felt Him tell me He had never left me – Christ who is so absolutely dependable, who would and could never let me down. Although I knew it was stupid to put your faith in any human being, the heart isn't always logical. But I knew there was forgiveness in my heart too for what my father had done. Christ also spoke to me of His Father who is mine also and who loved me more than any earthly father. Deeply moved, I experienced over the next few days a peace beyond anything I had ever felt before.

Wonderful as this inner healing was, there was more that God was wanting to achieve.

To explain this I must go back to that first night of prayer and pick up another strand that was interwoven with the rest of this story.

Later that night I went out in the car as I wanted to be on my own; but when I stopped somewhere quiet I had the disturbing feeling that my father was sitting next to me. Without my mentioning this to Grace the following week, she had felt an unexpected assault over the situation. During this second week, along with the peace described above there was also an increase of unpleasant activity from the enemy. In fact, at one point I felt him offer me the thing I had always wanted: to 'communicate' with my father. I was aghast, as I have always detested anything to do with the occult, and (not for the first time) a fear touched me.

When I spoke to Grace the third weekend, she asked what I felt about my father. I replied that, strangely, it was as if he had never existed. She asked if any of my father's side of the family had connections with the occult. Suddenly a great many things became clear. I knew my great-grandmother was involved in the occult; we both thought it likely that the same was true of my grandmother. This was confirmed by Diana, who had met my grandmother, and who joined Grace in ministering to me.[2]

Now that I knew what was coming against me I was a bit scared, but Grace and Diana told me to face the thing. As I did so, I could see it in spirit to my left. In wonder I saw Christ come to the right of me. I do not know how to describe Him. He just WAS: He WAS what He IS – and oh, the effect on this thing that was trying to make me afraid! It cowered in absolute terror of Christ! I don't remember seeing it go, but that's because I wasn't really interested. I wanted to look at Christ. I felt myself laugh with a glorious, jubilant triumph that I can feel even now as I write. Here was an aspect of Christ that I had known of and sensed from time to time but was now seeing for myself, and it was wonderful.

Since these experiences I have not been the same person. There is a feeling of starting all over again, as if at the edge of a vast ocean, with so much to explore. I am intensely grateful to God. He could have left me where I was (it was a good place), but He wants the best for His children. What touches me most is the desire I sensed in Christ for all of my heart. He had a lot of it, but wanted the inner citadel, and had pursued me for years to get this. I don't understand why He should want my love, but since then it has been increasingly His.

As for God's operating table, I wouldn't have swapped it for all the sofas in heaven!

This is the most recent testimonial to the 'new ministry' that was born in the Struthers Memorial group of churches in November 1994.[3] Jennifer's story shows something of the depth and power of God's moving since that time.

It had begun one weekend at our annual conference in High Wycombe in the south of England.. And for me it was not only a new beginning; it was part of the answer to a long-recognized need.

A Need Recognized

For many years I had felt an incompleteness in one realm of ministry. I did not always know how to handle the numbers who responded for personal ministry. On almost every excursion from home I faced this difficulty. At home I usually had the help of a well-trained team, but away from home I might see forty to over a hundred people rising for ministry and would have a very limited time to deal with them. I had always remembered Smith Wigglesworth, who one day learned the secret of the mass miracle, and I longed to have the same kind of thing happen for me. Preaching in Sweden, but forbidden by the authorities to lay on hands, he instructed the sick to lay their own hands on their heads as he prayed. God healed them that day in great numbers.[4]

You can picture me saying to God, 'Lord, when big numbers come out for deliverance, would you please deliver them all in a mass miracle?' God didn't say anything (either yea or nay), but He didn't do it. And I plodded on, case after case, through the weeks and the months and the years, feeling there must be something else.

The Action of God at High Wycombe

As I came into the meeting that night in High Wycombe, I had a strange feeling in my spirit, which I can't easily put into words, that God was doing or was about to do something unusual. I wanted to be very open to the action of the Spirit, to do just exactly what I was told. I wanted God to have His way.

Toward the end of the meeting I invited any whose needs had not been met in the afternoon to indicate their desire for help. As people responded, instead of taking them to another room or dividing them amongst the ministering team, I invited them to come to the front for ministry there. I knew by this time what I was about to do. There was a stirring within me now. There was the feeling, 'God is here.' There was a feeling of something new. And quite frankly I was spiritually experimenting. I knew I was going to pray for people this time as they stood.

You may think this was an obvious solution to my dilemma. Had not many across the world been 'slain in the Spirit' under anointed ministry? I had witnessed it myself in the case of Kathryn Kuhlman. But I am a very careful person in spiritual things and do not move with every wind that blows. I had always been aware of dangers, not with anything that God does, but dangers related to **us**, to what we are. Though I had seen wonderful miracles, I had also witnessed foolish things. I was well aware that if people were standing up for ministry, expecting to go down, and got to the point of balancing a little backward on their heels, they were almost halfway down already: I could understand the psychology of this. I had avoided any difficulty over the matter when praying with people by having them sit or kneel! (There were certainly people who did go prostrate where deliverance was concerned, but this was in a rather different category.) In short, I had long steered clear of the kind of ministry to which I was now being impelled.

Without knowing what would happen, I was open to the action of the Holy Spirit. As I put my hand on the head of the first of them, I think the phrase that I used was: *The anointing of the Holy.* I did not ask about their condition; my focus was not on them, but on God. 'Lord, what are You doing? What do You want to do? Lord, let the anointing of the Holy be upon them.' And suddenly, as in turn they received ministry, down on their backs they went. I got someone to stand behind each, because I sensed what was happening and didn't want them to be apprehensive at a natural level and have any concern about falling. So the first went down, and the second: *The anointing of the Holy* – down! *The anointing of the Holy* – down! One after another ... and not just struggling immediately to their feet, but remaining there for a time. Indeed when the meeting was finally over, there was one still there.

Without speaking privately to any of them or making any special selection, I got every one who was down to come and tell the company exactly what they felt God had done. As they spoke, my spirit was thrilling with the life of God.

One of them said, 'You know, your hand came on my head, but a force came against me and just pressed me right back; I had to go down.'

Another said, 'A demon came out of me as I lay on that floor.'

More than one spoke of being set free.

There was such a sense of the action of the Holy Spirit: not the ministry of man, but the action of God. Instead of being exhausted I was alive and full of energy. People did not need me to counsel them: they were in the hands of the living God.

Then I began to have a strong sensation that this was not a one-off occasion. This was the opening of a door to a realm that God wanted the church to come into, a realm that was not only for those with desperate needs who required to meet God, but also for those walking very well but needing a new touch of the Divine, a touch of the miraculous, a coming upon them of the hand of God. I was well aware that there had been meetings all over the country, often associated with the term 'the Toronto blessing' (although the Toronto Vineyard did not use that term themselves), where people claimed to have been blessed of God. I was also aware that people had been splitting left, right and centre over things that had happened in some of the gatherings.

But I believed that a wind of God was blowing in various parts of the world, and for us its effects were glorious. Yet while they may have been sensational from one point of view, there was not merely human excitement or hysteria, but often a great quietness. From the beginning I was interested not only in the phenomena associated with the blessing – but with what actually happens in the inner hearts of those who are prostrate before God. When God began a new movement in the High Wycombe conference I found that there was a very deep control, and a feeling of awe and glory in my spirit.

This sense of things was corroborated by one of the team members, **Diana**, in a report she gave on the conference the following weekend.

> On the Saturday night at the end of the service we went into a very rich tarry time, during which I prayed with a number of people while Pauline led worship.[5] Halfway through, Mr Black made an appeal for those who did not feel they had met God fully in earlier ministry to come to the front for

further help. A number of people responded. As he began to minister to them, from my position at the very back of the hall I could feel a tremendous power beginning to pour through him like waves of electricity. The lady with whom I was praying went down. Those at the front with whom Mr Black was praying began to go down one after the other, right down prostrate on the floor.

I have seen people going prostrate in the past; it has happened through my own ministry on a number of occasions. But there was something different this time that I hadn't felt before. The whole atmosphere became charged with the power of God, and a terribly strong feeling of His reality broke over the company, along with an awareness that He was ministering very, very deeply.

At the end of the meeting Mr Black, curious to know what had happened, invited those who had gone prostrate to come forward and testify. One after another spoke of being released or of feeling something break. One testimony in particular, I felt, was very real and alive; the one concerned kept saying, 'It's gone, it's gone! Praise God, it's gone!' Obviously in the space of thirty seconds something very real had happened.

This moving of God did seem to be something new, as Mr Black indicated at the end.

The Blessing Comes North

On returning from High Wycombe I explained to the fellowship in Scotland what had happened, feeling very strongly that God would continue to work in a similar way. My message to the company who gathered on Saturday night in Greenock was this:[6]

God, the great God of heaven, wants to meet you ... Prepare yourself to meet God. Prepare to pass from the level of thinking about that upper dimension to actually passing into it, as you come under the power of the Holy Spirit.

Many in the red sandstone church in West Stewart Street responded to the call that very evening. Five of them were asked afterwards to speak of their experience. One was **Ishbel**, a trained nurse and practising chiropodist, who had been the first to come forward.

I had had a sense of anticipation all day of coming to the meeting. When I answered the invitation to come forward and Mr Black put his hand towards me I felt an awareness of God, an awareness of the Spirit of Christ, a total acceptance in Him and an entering into Him in a deeper way.

I sat up after a while and He said, 'No, just stay there; I want you to stay in that place.'

Most of all I was conscious of Christ and the Spirit of God, and of His love and total provision for each one of us.

This theme of the love of God was strikingly echoed in the testimonies of two others. One was **Alan**, a doctor by profession.

It was with some reluctance that I stood up. I had put up my hand, thinking that maybe Mr Black would pray for us as we sat there. When he asked us to come out, I did not move at first. But I had no alternative but to obey God. I had even said, 'Well, look, God, if he gives a second appeal I'll go up.' That wasn't to be.

I almost thought I'd missed it – 'I can't go up now. Everybody's up.' There was no let-up, no get-out. Since Mr Black was just over at the side where I was, I thought, 'Maybe he'll take me now and I won't have to go right forward.' But that wasn't to be either.

I really wanted to be off the platform but was led there feeling very tense and fearful, I don't know quite why. Mr Black prayed with me; I don't even know if he put his hand on me; if he did it was extremely light. I felt it either just on my head or hovering slightly above it.

As I began to relax a bit, he spoke of the love of God, and the love of God in my life. And it's something that I don't find very easy to accept. I don't think of myself as a terribly lovely, or loving, or lovable, person. But my knees sort of gave way and I sank down. I didn't feel a great deal at first; I just felt still. I felt as though I had obeyed God, that I had done what He wanted. And I sensed that was enough. And as I speak now I do feel God's love come in in a new and different way, and I give Him thanks. Amen.

A gracious and kindly person (despite his own estimate of his self-worth!) Alan had been instrumental in helping one of his colleagues towards her discovery of Christ about six years earlier. **Anne** also was among those asked to testify, but was so overwhelmed by her experience of God's love that she could say very little at the time:

I just felt as Mr Black was speaking tonight that God was very, very close. I have been feeling very guilty recently about what a bad person I am, and I was having difficulty in believing that Jesus loved me. When Mr Black prayed with me just now, as I went down I felt a sense of warmth pass through my whole body, and a sense of the love of God and the love of Christ for me and for His people.

Many who knew her must have been surprised at the severity of her self-condemnation. Later she explained:

On the first occasion in Greenock when Mr Black spoke of the new ministry I felt very much affected by the presence of the Spirit. At the end he asked anyone who felt drawn into a new place to indicate so. I responded to this but, to be honest, when he went on to invite us to come to the front I really didn't want to go. After a struggle with myself I got up, thinking, 'If I feel this draw from the Spirit, I must do it.' I didn't really know what was going to happen, or exactly why there was such a draw to go for ministry.

When Mr Black started to pray I felt a powerful move of the Spirit, and went down on the floor. For a moment it seemed nothing happened. Had I made a mistake? But then a sense of warmth came over me, and a sense of God's love flooding my whole being.

The background to this was that for some time, and particularly in the two weeks leading up to that Saturday night, circumstances had arisen again and again, particularly at work, where my reactions were not at all as they should have been. At times I was angry and irritated, and it seemed that God was showing me things within which I hadn't fully appreciated were there. Having always thought I wasn't a terribly bad person, now I felt as if God was showing me otherwise – there were many things needing to be sorted out.

When God flooded me on the Saturday night with His love I sensed He was saying that although I couldn't understand how He could love me the way I was, yet He did, and not only did He love me, but that love was there for absolutely everyone. I felt deeply moved. It would be obvious to the gathering that I was quite overcome by the experience and found it very hard to speak.

There has been a difference since then. It is difficult to put it into words; but there is a settled peace, and a feeling that no matter what is within me, God can change it by His love. Praise His Name!

As Anne's narrative would suggest, one of the things that some people found difficulty with was the fact that God was meeting people in such love. He had come with great grace and gentleness to set people free, and was not as severe on some as they thought He would be. He can come with iron and a sword, but He can come differently at different times to different people.

To **Julia**, who is herself a very gentle person and a lover of beauty, He came with a revelation of His power. In her own words:

> The power of God is very strong up here. When I came up to sing in the choir earlier tonight I could feel it on the platform area, and at one point I sensed an electricity when Mr Black was talking. And so when he called people forward I felt that I should go because I could feel the Lord touching me – I could feel the anointing. When I came forward I could feel the power on the platform. And I didn't really know what to expect. But when Mr Black touched me, the power came into my spirit, and I know that God has strengthened me and has given me a revelation of His power.
>
> And it's awesome, it's awesome! But it carries you away to a deeper place in Him, and there's fire in it, and power in it, and anointing. That was the word that came to me first when I was touched, and I thought, 'This is Your **anointing**.' It's like fire, and it's glory; it is a revelation of the glory of God! And it is a wonderful and a strengthening thing.
>
> Oh, the power of the Son of God that is in it! I am holding on to this lectern because I can hardly stand up for the power.

There was nothing stereotypical about these experiences. God was touching individuals personally. To **Isa**, a frequent visitor to 'Saturday nights at Struthers', He seems to have come in a way that she had glimpsed from outside but never tasted for herself. She told her story with disarming simplicity:

> 'Do you ever feel that someone else has got something that you've not got?'
>
> When the speaker said this at a Woman's Aglow meeting this morning, it summed up the feeling I have when I come to Struthers on a Saturday night. I am a regular member of another church and very much involved in its activities. Yet when the word is preached on Saturday nights, I am taken away up to another realm, and I think, 'I've not got that.'
>
> To a friend I often say, 'Do you ever feel that you are not really like the people in there?'
>
> I had wanted to go forward for prayer this morning at the Aglow meeting, but was engaged at the bookstall.
>
> But it was Saturday, and I knew I was to come to the meeting in Struthers. Sitting there I felt the Lord speaking to me, but didn't think for a moment that I was going to have the opportunity to be prayed with. I don't even remember walking forward. Lying down there, I thought I was dead and had gone to heaven, because all I could hear was heavenly angels singing round me! And I praise God!

And so with power and gentleness God came to His people. But it was only the beginning. We were to learn more of what had happened that night when others testified later. And in the weeks and months that followed, God continued to move in ways that were not only outwardly sensational but also dramatic and permanent in their effects.

The following chapters recount the experiences of others who encountered God in many different ways as they lay on the carpet under His anointing.

Notes

[1] My daughter Grace Gault is in charge of our Greenock (West Stewart Street) church. She has contributed material to my *Revival: Living in the Realities* (New Dawn Books, 1993), and *War in Heaven and Earth* (New Wine Press, 1996).

[2] Diana Rutherford leads the Cumbernauld branch of our fellowship. For her contributions to earlier publications, see, for example, my *Gospel Vignettes* (New Dawn Books, 1989) and *War in Heaven and Earth*.

[3] It should be explained that the Struthers Memorial group of churches consists of churches and fellowship groups scattered across the United Kingdom. The 'mother' church is based in West Stewart Street, Greenock, where some of our general church conferences are still held. Each of our branches has its own leader; my own oversight extends to all.

[4] More detailed accounts of this story appear in Stanley H. Frodsham, *Smith Wigglesworth, Apostle of Faith* (Elim Publishing Co., 1949), pp. 40–1, 72.

[5] The reference is to Pauline Anderson, now in charge of our fellowship in the London area. Her story is told in my book *The Incomparable Christ* (New Dawn Books, 1989).

[6] 'Saturday nights in Struthers', to which allusion is frequently made in this book, were held in Greenock until early 1995, when they were transferred to our church in Glasgow.

Chapter 2

From Glory to Glory

Were you to ask what was the hallmark of the 'new' ministry, it would be too easy to point to the numbers who went prostrate. This was indeed an outer indication of something that God was doing, and was potently reinforced by the fruits in the lives of those who had met God in this way. These included cleansing and power over sin, physical and emotional healing, increase of love amongst the people, and strength for everyday living. But most of all there was a tremendous access through the Spirit to Christ and to God Himself: there was an atmosphere emanating from the holy place which was felt by individuals as they were taken 'within the veil'. It was out of this atmosphere that there was generated the variety of visible phenomena, and it was into this atmosphere that God's people were most poignantly drawn.

Something of this is conveyed in the following testimony from **Elaine**, who runs her own physiotherapy clinic in the west end of Greenock:

> The Sunday morning meeting in Glasgow was probably one of the most beautiful meetings that I have ever been in. The sense of the presence of God that was there was absolutely glorious. In the communion time Mary began to minister to us.[1] As she prayed I went down, and I felt the Holy Spirit all around me.

To begin with I wondered what God would say to me and what He would do. And I felt to relax into His presence and not worry about trying to find God but just let Him come right in. As I relaxed, an amazing peace came over my being. It was with a tremendous sense of joy that I realized there was no barrier between God and me, and that I could go out and out into heaven. Wave upon wave of worship started to go over my being.

As I was lying there I almost wondered how far to go with it. I remember Pauline Anderson speaking about being free, and how far can you go in this?[2] People don't normally make any noise when they're on the ground; they're normally quiet and lie still and they don't generally speak in tongues or do very much. But I felt a tremendous draw to go right out in worship and in song. I thought, 'God, is this all right? Can I do this?' And this very strong thought came to me: *Just go with it. You might never have another opportunity, and life is too short. I'm here right now to bless you, and heaven is open for you right here and now – take the opportunity that I'm giving to you.* And so I went with the Holy Spirit as far as I could, and as I was lying there I was tremendously aware of worship and of heaven, and also of the sense of God that was in the meeting. There was a beautiful, beautiful sense of unity amongst the people and of love going up from many, many hearts.

After some time I became aware of somebody nearby. For a long time there had been a barrier between this person and myself. I had tried over several years to sort the matter and had earnestly looked for opportunity to get it right before God and with the one concerned. But the opportunity never arose. I never really knew what the problem was, and in my mind I knew it was stupid, because we both wanted the same thing; we both wanted God, and we both wanted to see souls saved; we just wanted God. I was aware of the person there, and there was suddenly this incredible desire through my heart: 'O God, could You just sort this now?' I felt I wanted to reach out my hand to her and take hold of her hand. Then I thought, 'You can't do that – we don't do that!' I felt Mr Black would be saying, 'We'll have none of the flesh in here!'

Lest the reader be misled by Elaine's sense of humour, I am less of an ogre than this suggests! It is when things get out of hand that I am troubled: when for example a service is repeatedly interrupted by the necessity of every late-comer's receiving a hug from the chairman. I don't think that some of the things that happen are sensible, to put it mildly. But when there is a genuine moving of God, a hug can be a very lovely expression of it. I told Elaine to put her inhibitions at rest and hug anybody she liked ... except me!

Then I thought, 'Well, life's too short, and Mr Black's not here! And I don't know when ever I'll feel like this again, and You're moving now.'

I opened my eyes (and fortunately she had her eyes open too) and reached up my hand, and I don't know what she thought, but as I reached up she came and knelt down beside me. I didn't know what to say ... and so I simply said, 'Could you just stay there a minute?' And I shut my eyes and went into God. There was a terrible, terrible grief; the pain and tears came right over my spirit and I sobbed and cried with the pain of it, and the wounding of it all. Then I felt God check and say, 'Now, go right into Me – right out into the Spirit.' And as I did that and pushed my spirit right out into God, it was as though a bolt of the fire of love passed through me and into her. It was, I think, just the love of God that came.

I don't really know all that she felt. We both kind of cried again, and then suddenly this peace came. It was the most beautiful peace I think I've ever felt, right round about us. The atmosphere was thick with the presence of God and the peace that was there. I could have stayed there for ever. That peace of God held us together in spirit, and there was love and unity between us. The whole difficulty was completely healed. And I knew that God had done an absolute miracle. After a while I sat up. Feeling a bit embarrassed, I thought, 'I wonder what she'll say?' She just threw her arms around me – and we don't normally do that either! But God was there, and we both rejoiced together in how good it was to be in the place of unity, and how pleasant it is for the brethren to dwell in unity. I think I turned to her and said, 'This is revival – this is revival.' And I believe it is.

Elaine's testimony illustrates a significant feature of God's dealing with lives at this time. It was what might be called the 'layered' quality of spiritual experiences. First He might come in love, and in the sweetness of that visitation He would reveal a further area requiring attention, and then again His love would flow in.

We see this pattern in the case of **Tony**, a computer systems consultant, two of whose experiences are recounted here:

After Mr Black prayed with me one Sunday night in Glasgow, for part of the time that I was down I felt the sweetness of Christ very close to me. The interesting thing was that nothing specific seemed to happen: while I felt really touched by God, I couldn't put my finger on anything and say, 'This is what happened to me tonight,' although it was a wonderful experience.

I went to Greenock the following night and gave testimony to that effect. Right from the start of the meeting I felt very free and 'through' to God. During the prayer time we were really worshipping, and all of a sudden I seemed to be above the room looking down on it. I could see myself, and I saw Jesus come towards me and hold out His hand.

He said, 'Take my hand.'

I said, 'I can't,' and in fact I saw myself cry and turn away from Him. He said it again, and again; I had to turn my back on Him and say, 'I can't.'

Watching this, I asked, 'Well, why can't I do it? What's wrong?'

He said one word: 'Shame.'

Just for a moment I felt despair. I thought, 'Surely there's not yet another barrier stopping me getting through to God.'

And again, as I was looking down at this thing, God said, 'Look at the light.'

This sounds strange, I know, but right in front of me was a big tube, and I knew it was full of light. It started to turn from a vertical position down towards me so that I could see into it as it came down. There was fire coming out of it all round the rim, and in the centre was the brightest light. As it came down I knew I was scared to look at it, and yet something inside was saying, 'Look at the light. I'm not afraid to look at the light.'

It turned and it turned until it came directly in front of me. I don't know what happened then, but the next thing was that this vision went and I was back sitting in the Greenock hall again.

I felt Jesus right beside me, and He said, 'Put your hand out and take My hand.'

Physically I put my hand out, and I knew He put His hand in mine. Though I didn't see it, I knew it was there, and that if I'd put my other hand on top I would have had His hand between my two hands. I felt I was free before this experience; but afterwards it was just tremendous – as though heaven opened, and came pouring down. It just felt so, so free!

He never did say what I was ashamed of. Without going into the detail of it, He just named the obstacle and took it away. It was really amazing; praise His Name.

One of the wonderful things to which these two testimonies point is that God is never finished working with us. There is no end to the realm into which He would take us. One of the greatest dangers in the Christian life is complacency: the most mature of us cannot afford to be content with what God has provided for yesterday's banquet, no matter how rich.

An example was the case of one lady who had not yet come to terms with the new ministry, but nevertheless had a wonderful encounter with God. She could so easily have rested satisfied with what she had, imagining there could be nothing better. As **Diana Rutherford**, who ministered to her, tells the story:

A lady had come from a different church where many people had gone prostrate in the past. She had never been open to this ministry and had felt at times pushed. Nor had she liked it when similar manifestations had come into our own gathering. A very shy and self-conscious person, she had certain reservations. She became quite shadowed because in her fear she had closed off to that ministry and indeed to the church. I chatted the problem through with her one day and told her to forget all about it and just to go into the Spirit as she normally did in a meeting, and not to think about people going down under the power, or about herself going down either.

In the Sunday night meeting that week she went through to God and found herself coming into a place of worship that she had never touched before.

She said to me, 'I feel as though I have found a new place in God. I don't think there is a better place to be in; it is lovely. I can't possibly have any more.'

But, you know, in the very next meeting she attended I felt the Holy Spirit indicate to me to go and pray with her and she would go down. I hesitated. Part of me felt, 'Lord, she's just come to accept this, barely within forty-eight hours. Would it not be better to give her more time to come to terms with it all?'

Feeling the Holy Spirit draw me, I went to her. And she went down beautifully under the anointing of the Holy Spirit. She fell almost in slow motion and went out in the Spirit into the glory of God. I stayed with her for a time just to watch and to be with her. In her own words, she felt she was at the doorway of heaven. She had never experienced anything like it before. She thought she had got as much as she could possibly get on the Sunday night, and here she was going out further.

She has spoken to me since and talked of the pain in her heart. She cannot view life in the same way again. Relationships with other people have changed because she is looking at them now through the eyes of Christ. She has seen the glory, and she can never again be the same.

Glory be to God.

Another who found God dealing with her in more than one way on successive occasions was **Janet**, a senior physiotherapist who was suffering from burn-out at the start of the new ministry in Struthers. Almost without any movement on Janet's part God healed her body and mind; but there was a more important operation to follow, requiring deep preparation, for her spirit. As she explained later:

Nineteen-ninety-four was the busiest year of my entire life. It was also one of the most stressful. Towards the end of November I more or less cracked. Those closest to me knew just how close that point came.

It was around that time that Mr Black came back from High Wycombe and there was the beginning of the new ministry amongst us. One Saturday night after listening to a testimony to healing I considered going forward for ministry.

'Lord,' I thought, 'I need a miracle. I'm stuck; I can't cope; I can't go on any longer. Physically and spiritually I'm burnt out.'

And just as I was sitting there, God opened the dimension that Mr Black had been speaking about. Something inside radically changed; when I got up on the Sunday morning I knew it. Something happened to me that would normally have taken many months. People who suffer from burn-out do not recover quickly. Yet the healing came very, very quietly. After months of strain, I felt back to being me.

With her medical background, Janet had reason to appreciate the miraculous nature of the healing she received. But that was not all:

Thinking that was the matter finished, I was grateful to God, because I had got myself into a mess and He had got me out of it really quickly.

And then one night at the end of the year God said, 'I haven't finished yet.'

I knew His speaking was connected to the new movement of His Spirit in our midst, but for some time did not form any further opinions on it, until during one Saturday night meeting in the middle of January I thought, 'What should I do about this?' Having been very aware of the depth of the presence of God that had come with the new ministry, I had no hang-ups about it. Most people seemed to feel that they had to think about it first! But I wasn't very sure what my personal response should be. Sitting there I felt a degree of confusion.

Suddenly God said to me, 'It's all right. I'll tell you what you need to know, and I'll tell you when you need to respond: stop worrying about it.'

A week later again I asked the question, 'What do I do here?'

God said, 'Go home and prepare your soul.' And I knew very definitely that I should go for ministry the following night in Glasgow.

As I began to prepare myself late on the Saturday night for what would happen, I found that the sense of the awe of the presence of God came into my house for just a few minutes. On the Sunday I was nervously aware of the fact that God was moving towards the operation. In the morning meeting there was a far deeper access than I had had for a long time in spiritual places. When it came to the meeting at night I went forward for ministry, and Mr Black said one sentence to me, which I have no intention of revealing – but it echoed what was in my head! The same covering and the same sense of awe of God's presence came over me as at home the previous night. I knew that I would not get away with staying on my feet. God intended me to go down before Him, and that's exactly what happened.

I don't understand it; there's no way I could say I understand it. But there was the awe of His presence, and the covering of the blood of Christ over my whole being. Something was completed (as I knew it would be) by my obedience in preparing and in going forward for ministry because God said, 'Do it.' The inner healing and strength that came with it was confirmed. Such was the depth of the presence of God over the next few days that I could hardly wait to get to the next Saturday night meeting!

Janet went on to ruminate about the incongruity of her very conventional religious upbringing and her more recent situation on the floor:

It struck me that the experience was not something I would necessarily have enjoyed at a natural level. In my very respectable earlier church background this kind of thing is just not done and would have been severely criticized. In fact, one night when my mum arrived at the meeting (after it was over, fortunately!) I thought, 'If she could have seen what was going on in here, she'd have had a fit, with all these people lying on the floor!' But such is the sense of the presence of God, and such is the access to God in it, that you don't think about things like that any more; you just let the bonds break.

I am aware that there are many Christians under this kind of constraint, feeling that 'one doesn't do this' in respectable churches. You might never have come forward for ministry because of that; you might not be able to face it. Perhaps it is not something you have consciously thought about. But you are not responding, because you think, 'This isn't for me; I can't do that because I'm not that kind of person.' I have become keenly aware this is for everybody. There is an access to God, and to the power and the anointing that comes with it, for everybody.

I don't know how long I was lying on the floor in Glasgow – I don't really care. But the sense of the presence of God and the access into His presence! For some people all that is needed is straightforward obedience. It was willingness and obedience to move when God spoke that gave Him access and brought the change for me. Since then there has been a completeness inside and a moving forward.

Janet then refers to a scriptural promise given to the church at the beginning of 1995.[3]

I have found that the New Year Word, which was speaking volumes beforehand, is so constantly before me that I can't think of anything else at all. Every time I turn myself towards God it lives in real power. I think all these things are tied up together.

I praise God for what He has done. Without His action I would have cracked; but the power of God has come and brought a real, deep inner healing.

Janet's testimony brings out an important emphasis: it is on the element of obedience. She was open, she was waiting on God to know what to do, and when He told her, she did it. In His own appointed time and way, He came. In the words of the song that came to us at that time:

> Come, Holy Spirit, we await You:
> Come in all Your sovereign power;
> This is the day the Lord has chosen,
> This is the day and this the hour.

As we sang these words, again and again their truth became manifest before our eyes. Often, indeed, He came gloriously on the wings of song – whether in English or in tongues, as 'the Spirit Himself gave utterance'. The anointing that was in the atmosphere fell on the congregational worship also, so that often what was happening on the floor at the front of the church was going unnoticed by those who were moving out in the Spirit where they were sitting or standing. And the songs that were born at this time carried the hallmark of the new anointing.

Notes

[1] The reference is to my daughter Mary Black, who is in charge of our Glasgow congregation. Her testimony is in chapter 4 of my *Christian Fundamentals* (New Dawn Books, 1991), one of whose appendices is also written by her.

[2] Compare the experience Pauline describes in *Christian Fundamentals*, p. 73.

[3] See chapter 9 for a general explanation of this annually expected 'word' or 'promise'. The promise for 1995 was given in Isaiah 1:18–19 and Psalm 132:13–16.

Chapter 3

The Coming of Song:
A Wind from Lindisfarne

It was a glorious day – as beautiful as summer though it was late November. We were on Lindisfarne, the famous 'Holy Isle' and early centre of Christianity off the coast of Berwickshire. The other members of the family, as I knew, wanted to walk. There were lots of walking opportunities, and I let all of them pass me by. I don't walk too much nowadays!

There had come a strange thought as we were travelling. Through the years, when I have gone from home there has almost always been something to do for God, somebody to see – and in fact, it can be quite a joke because, as you will appreciate, it can interfere a little with more mundane pursuits. But I suddenly found myself thinking, 'This is strange. I have nothing in particular to do for God.' I was totally relaxed; I was reading a very interesting book as we stopped from place to place, and normally when I get hold of that kind of book I read on and on. I was part way through it when we got to Lindisfarne. And I felt something happen. My spirit was probing out into the spiritual world and pondering the things that God had been doing.

My spirit was in action. And there came the thought: 'Write a hymn.' From a human point of view, if I had been stopping I would have got on with my book or a newspaper, but I had no desire to pursue this.

In my earlier days I did sometimes write a little poetry – but not seriously for years.

'Write a hymn.' And I began to write. I had a strange, strange feeling. A great part was written almost straight; almost without correction or alteration or anything like that. There was a feeling of receiving revelation. I went with the revelation, and I thought, 'Well, that's that.' Then it was as though He said, 'But I want this, and this, to go in.' And I opened myself and worked away, until I felt a sense of at least comparative completion.

On my return home I came into our church bookshop in the morning and a friend asked kindly if I'd had a pleasant time: what did I do?

'Oh,' I said, 'I wrote a hymn.' And she laughed me almost out of the shop.

'You wrote a hymn?' She seemed to think that because I'm not a golden-voiced singer I (obviously) couldn't possibly write a hymn.[1]

I said, 'Yes, I wrote a hymn. I'll read it to you.' I had it in my hand.

Her jaw dropped. 'Oh,' she said, 'that's lovely,' or words to that effect. She looked at me. 'I didn't think you **could** write a hymn!'

Well, oddly enough, I don't have the feeling of having written the hymn I am about to introduce. There is rather the feeling of something of God coming through. And I want to take you to the innerness of it, as I took my congregation, step by step:

> Come, Holy Spirit, we await You:
>   Come in all Your sovereign power;
> This is the day the Lord has chosen,
>   This is the day and this the hour.

You want to get into your spirit that waiting attitude: not to go brashly in 'and we'll have this kind of singing and that kind of singing and we'll bring the blessing down and glory be to God...' 'Come, Holy Spirit: **we** await **You.**' This brings us into the right attitude at the very beginning. We await the Holy Spirit, remembering who God is: His sovereignty, His power.

The second couplet came to me very strangely. Beyond the reflectiveness in the hymn, there is the action of God. I believe that this hour is chosen of God. This day is in the calendar of God to move upon the churches all across the land. He is coming again and again in many ways in different churches just now, to those who are prepared to await the coming of the Spirit. 'This is the day and this the hour.' It has the triumph in it of the conquering Son of God. Its tone and attitude are reminiscent of the well-known lines, 'The Son of God goes forth to war, a kingly crown to win.'

> Come, gentle Spirit, we await You:
>   Come in all Your holy grace;
> Show us now the things of Jesus,
>   Show to us now His blessed face.

And I had a feeling of the very gentleness of Christ, the gentleness of God, in this particular moving. He is coming very gently, He is coming as a dove, not crashing in (in a particular way). There is power, but there is also the grace of the Lord Jesus, the grace and gentleness of the Spirit. You remember the connection: *'He shall take of the things that are Mine and He shall reveal them unto you'* (cf. John 16:14). Take, Holy Spirit, the things of Jesus. Isn't that our desire and our prayer?

> Come, Holy Spirit, we can feel You
>   Falling on us like a shower;
> Bless we now the Name of Jesus,
>   Thrill we now with holy power.

41

Come, Holy Spirit, we can sense You
  Coming like the gentle rain;
Love a mantle falling on us –
  Sing we now our glad refrain.

Then I felt God turn my attention to some of the things
the Holy Spirit would do in the midst of us. There is the
singing to Him, the giving praise to God, but there is the
work that the Holy Spirit wants to accomplish as we are
on the floor or in our seats or wherever we may be.

Take the things that shade His glory:
  Pierce the clouds that lie between;
Convict of sin, O Holy Spirit,
  That His glory may be seen.

Yes, convict of sin. He can do it very gently, but ask
Him to do it, to convict wherever that is needed.

Come, Holy Spirit, to release us:
  Bind our wounds and set us free;
Break the cruel bands of darkness
  As Thy glorious light we see.

Lift the burdens, Holy Spirit,
  Heal the scars and staunch the pain
By the precious blood of Jesus,
  Through the Lamb who once was slain.

Sing we now the song of Jesus,
  Praise we now the stricken Lamb;
Unctioned by the Holy Spirit,
  Praise we now the great I AM.

As we approached the time of ministry, I counselled the
congregation:

Shall we prepare ourselves to go on to the operating
table of God? That is as I see the experience: coming

on to that operating table, that He might do with us exactly as He wishes to do, that we may feel His presence, and get as close to Him as we possibly can.

It was necessary to reassure people that the new was not by any means a denial of the old. Someone had actually wondered if the new ministry had made me a 'different' person – could they talk to me as they used to do? Well, well!

One of the most nervous in her initial response to the introduction of the new ministry was **Sarah**, who from her seat at the very front of the congregation had a prime view of all that was going on. Used to working with the handicapped, Sarah could handle many of life's emergencies with aplomb – but the sight of people falling all around her in God's house was too much:

> On the first night of the new ministry I had been really frightened at what was going on at the front of the church. All through the prayer time, as people were falling all around me, I sat gripping my seat and crying my eyes out, because I couldn't understand what was happening or why it was happening in our church.

But through the week Sarah felt the peace of God coming into her again, and the knowledge grew that the only way she would lose her fear was to come out for prayer herself. This she did on the following Friday night in Glasgow – the occasion on which I told the people of my visit to Lindisfarne and the writing of the 'Song of Jesus'. Describing what had happened to her that night, Sarah continued:

> At the start of the service I was very nervous, because I knew that if an appeal was made that night to go out for prayer I would have to go forward. During the singing at the beginning I felt as if I was under a big

black cloud of sin and unworthiness: how could I possibly draw nigh to God? I found myself praying, 'God, cover me with Your blood. If You don't cover me with Your blood, I can't come through into this place.' And just as I was praying that, I had an almost physical sense of the covering of the blood coming upon my body.

The preaching came and went, and Mr Black invited people who wanted prayer to come out. I sat there and struggled. While my mind was saying, 'You know, you can't possibly go out there,' another part of me was saying, 'But this presence of the Holy Spirit is so strong upon me, how can I stay in my seat?'

Normally Mr Black gives only one appeal for ministry, and by this time he had prayed with many others. Thinking I was quite safe, I said to God, 'Well, if You want me to go out for prayer, then You have to ask him to say it again.' Unbelievably, Mr Black stood right in front of me and said, 'Anybody who feels God speaking to them, come out for prayer!' So I jumped out of my seat, expecting to get prayed with down at the front – but he led me right on to the platform. The tears were running down my face, because I was so scared of what was going to happen to me. My mind was persistently niggling: 'What are you doing? Here you are out on this platform! What's going to happen to you?'

Just as Mr Black was coming towards me (before he came anywhere near me) it was as if a sort of tube came right down over me and the mantle of the Holy Spirit fell upon me. In that presence of the Holy Spirit I knew that this was of God, and I knew that it was God Himself who was doing this work. Mr Black laid his hand on my head so gently that I think he almost wouldn't have needed to do it; the Holy Spirit had come upon me. I haven't a clue what Mr Black said, or what he prayed. The next thing I remember is lying flat out on the floor.

My mind was still active, and one part of me was saying, 'Sarah, you are lying on the floor, on the platform of the Glasgow church, and the church is full!'

The minute that had passed through my mind, my spirit just jumped and said, 'I don't care!'

As I lay there, the presence of God deepened and deepened. First of all there was a joy, and then I was crying, and again there was joy, and then there was an absolute peace.

I think the congregation had begun to sing at the time. As the music seemed to get louder in the congregation it faded out from my hearing and the place went deeply silent. I was so aware of the presence of God; it was as if Christ Himself had come to me. Just as that happened, I found that the words coming from me were, 'Oh, Christ, it's You!' I had been frightened of being struck down by a bolt of lightning – I just didn't know what was going to happen. And in that place it was the Christ that I knew when I sat in my seat, it was the Christ that I knew who walked with me every day, it was that Christ who came to me. It wasn't somebody I didn't know, it wasn't a presence that I didn't recognize, and it wasn't something that I was afraid of. The minute the mantle of the Holy Spirit fell upon me, all fear left, and I became so aware of the presence of Christ. All around me was love and peace.

I don't fully understand what happened last night. I don't fully understand the effect that it has had on my life. But I know that something inside is different, and something has opened up to God. A peace has come in that I never knew before, and a knowledge that Christ loves me and that He is not out to frighten us. He is not wanting to strike us all down and terrify us into doing His will and living a pure life. He came ever so gently to me – He Himself came upon me, and in that place I was unafraid; a real light and purity came within me, and all the fear of not being able to draw near to God passed away, and instead I became aware of the blood of Christ and its power. Covered in that blood I was safe; I was safe in the arms of Jesus. I didn't feel I was shielded from an angry and an awesome God; I was rather wrapped around by His love and held in a place of absolute security, a place of peace, a place of love, and a place where He Himself had come to me very quietly and very gently and had showed me Himself again in a completely different way from anything I have ever known before.

It was not uncommon for people to have very real experiences that the mind could not immediately (if ever) explain. Sarah's perception that something in her had 'opened up to God' was fully justified by the events that followed as she received further ministry over the next few months. She was to find inner healing from a childhood hurt and misplaced sense of guilt that had lodged deep in her psyche; long-sought healing of a relationship; increasing revelation of Christ's love and a confirmation of God's call on her life. The story of these events is continued in the second book of this trilogy.

Note

[1] It should perhaps be mentioned that I did not write the tune for this (or any) hymn! That was done by another.

Chapter 4

`Healing Power

Lift the burdens, Holy Spirit,
   Heal the scars and staunch the pain
By the precious blood of Jesus,
   Through the Lamb who once was slain.

When I spoke of 'the operating table of God', as I frequently did, I was not referring in particular to physical healing. But a large category of those who came under the ministrations of the Divine Surgeon did in fact receive bodily healing. This chapter relates three notable examples.

One night in May 1995 while ministering to someone I suddenly became aware of a drama going on at my back. At the centre of it was **Margaret M**, a relative of one of our Glasgow congregation. The victim of two strokes, Margaret had been awaiting ministry at the front. She was blind to the extent that she could not read a book, and walking was so difficult that she was due to have a hip replacement. That was the condition in which she came staggering out to the front, hardly able to stand. She recapitulates:

> I don't know where I had left my stick. I was trying to come down by holding on to the ends of the pews.

Then Mr Black asked us to line up in front of the platform. Now I couldn't stand without holding on: I had to have my stick, or lean against something. Since there was nothing there to lean on to, my legs started to shake.

Poor Margaret! While she had been waiting with others at the front, I had happened to see in the prayer line one of our friends who had been healed of a phobia of drowning, and had asked her to testify where she stood. As a result, the company standing there were kept rather longer than usual before anyone ministered. Margaret struggled to remain on her feet:

'Steady up,' I thought. Then I prayed, 'Lord, You've brought me this length. Stay with me and let me lean on You; don't let me fall.'

But I did fall! Two hands were laid on my shoulders, and I went right down.

While lying on the floor I felt as though someone had put their hands behind my ankle, and very gently but firmly pulled both my legs. At the same time, going across my eyes were (as it seemed) fingers of crystal with a bright light behind – the colours were breathtakingly beautiful. I could hear the congregation singing but felt I was lying within a circle on my own, and the voices had become very quiet.

I seemed to know when it was time to get up, and so I sat up and looked around. I was a bit fuzzy and didn't know just where I was going. When I started to stand up, someone came forward and asked me, 'Can I help you?'

I said, 'No, I'm all right, thank you,' and proceeded to look for my seat.

But oh, this pounding of my heart, and the joy that was through me! I wanted to laugh and I wanted to cry – I didn't know what I wanted to do! Unable to find my seat, I walked up the aisle until someone came out and said, 'You were sitting there, Margaret,' and plonked me down!

It's still so exciting! I sat down with the tears running down my face, and yet I was laughing. I thought, 'Oh, I better get up and out of here.'

So I stood up, and there was Moira at the end of the row.

She said, 'Margaret, what's happened?'

'Oh, Moira, I don't know.'

She said, 'I was walking behind you on the way down, and your poor legs were so swollen and they looked so painful. Now you're dancing up the aisle!'

'Oh,' I said, 'I know. Moira, come and have a cup of tea. I'm shaking all over.'

We went out into the coffee shop and stood where all the cards were on show. I don't know what made me do it, but I picked up a card and opened it ... **and I started to read what was on the card**.

Incredulously, I kept saying to Moira, 'Moira, I can read!'

She said, 'So what?' She didn't know anything about my eyes – very few people did!

'Come on,' she said, 'sit down there and have your tea.' As I started to sip my tea Moira put her hand over to where the books were.

Pulling a book over, she said, 'Right, see if you can read that.'

And I did – a whole page. Tears and all, I was reading!

'Margaret, that's so wonderful,' she said. 'Go and tell Mr Black.'

I said, 'If I go just now I'll pass out; I'm too excited!'

Not wanting to get the book in a mess, I turned it over to close it and put it down – and, praise the Lord, the title was *The Happiest People on Earth*! That night I was the happiest person!

I praise His holy Name and give credit to Christ for what He has done for me.

Margaret's voice was still tremulous with joy throughout this account, given a week after her experience.

That experience had perhaps been even more wonderful than she knew. I remember what happened very clearly. After ministry commenced I suddenly felt someone bumping into my back. It was in fact Margaret. I turned round just in time to see someone helping to catch her before she fell.

Margaret told me that from her point of view, two hands on her shoulders pushed her quietly down. Now no human hands touched her. I happen to know this. She was not prayed for in the normal way. My hands never came on her. Nor (so far as we can find) did anyone pull her legs! Now she no longer needed a hip replacement. Where her eyes were concerned, we were in the presence of the healing of an irreversible condition. The hand of the Lord was upon her.

I felt great delight in the knowledge that God had in fact done the very thing that Christ spoke about so long ago: *The deaf hear, the lame walk, the blind have sight restored, and the poor have the good tidings preached.* He is the same yesterday, today and for ever. We needed no hype, we needed no false human excitement. Only let there be the deep moving of the Holy Spirit, and the miracles were right there.

* * * * *

One of the early instances was **Comfort**, a busy wife and mother, who came with several ailments. Knowing nothing of the new ministry that had just come into the church, she had asked God if He would heal her of just one of her troubles. To her astonishment He did far more than that.

For some time I had felt there were too many difficult situations in my life. They included bodily pain of many kinds. One Monday I was in despair and was praying. While I was reading the Bible with somebody, we saw that there the Lord did not turn anybody away from healing.

I said, 'Oh ... then how come everybody doesn't get healed?'

Then the Lord ministered instantaneously that for some His grace is sufficient. I decided that I would still pray, and then if the Lord said that His grace was sufficient I would leave it at that.

So from Monday to Thursday I prayed, and I told my husband to pray, that I would have one of the situations in my life relieved. Since I was taking water tablets for swelling on the foot, I said, 'Well, Lord, if I can stop taking the water tablets, that's sufficient for me. I can bear all the other pains.'

By Thursday my spirit was rising. There was the urge: 'Go on praying – by faith you will receive.' The Bible says that if you are ill you should seek the elders to pray for you. In April this year Mr Black had prayed for me about migraine. Though I didn't tell him what happened afterwards, I had got healed of my migraine. So I hoped it wouldn't be too much to ask again for one of my physical troubles to be healed.

On Friday I thought, 'I don't have transport to Greenock.'

But as it happened, between twelve and one o'clock on Saturday a friend of mine turned up at the door and said, 'I am going to Greenock. Would you come?'

And it's as if the Lord just said, 'Here you are. You wanted Greenock; you wanted Mr Black; here is the transport.'

I managed to cancel another engagement for the evening and came with my friend to Greenock.

When I heard Mr Black saying something about a new movement of God, I was reminded of another meeting in Edinburgh to which I had gone and had not been slain in the Spirit. Rather than go for this kind of ministry again, I thought I would wait till the end of the service and then go to him for prayer. But halfway through the preaching there was the knowledge, 'I have to go now.' So as he finished preaching, by the time he called people I was at the front; I don't know how I got there. I stood at the front while other people were being prayed for, until he got to me.

Then I think my human mind came in to cause confusion: 'Oh, maybe if you don't fall you won't get healed ... You didn't fall in Edinburgh, so you won't fall here.' While Mr Black had his hands on my head and was praying, I tried to stabilize my concentration, but I didn't hear what he said because of my mental battle over being slain in the Spirit. Then he left, and I thought if I wasn't falling, I should go to my seat.

Just before I did that my two feet went so fast from under me that next thing I was on the floor. I thought, 'Oh! I'm now on the floor! So what's happening next?' Two people had given testimony and had told how the overpowering action of the Holy Spirit came upon them, and I wondered, 'How is it going to be over-powering?' I was expecting something so dramatic. And then – nothing happened.

As I lay there, I remembered the first line of the hymnsheet we had used earlier. I said, 'Come, Holy Spirit, I await You.'

Suddenly I felt a warm burning sensation coming from my feet. Within me I was thinking, 'But this is gentle.'

And then it came up and up and up, and got to my chest. At this point I realized that something was happening, because it felt as though a little hammer was knocking on my chest within. And I said, 'What's happening in my heart?'

That was the first communication.

'I'm healing you,' He said. 'I am the Lord that healeth thee.' He reminded me that there had been a sprained muscle for nearly fourteen years in the region of my heart, caused by childbirth. I got frightened, and I said, 'Oh!'

And then the hammering stopped and went on to my sinus. I didn't actually pray for my sinus, but I started feeling a sensation like when you rub methylate on your nose and feel it melting through to your throat.

That was when I actually felt the depth of what was happening, and I said, 'Lord – but I was asking only for my feet!'

It's strange: though I'd had the migraine healing, I thought that was maybe a one-off thing. But when I started feeling so many things within me I was amazed. I was lying there smiling, but also getting anxious.

I thought, 'Can the Lord do this? Is this the Lord that we cannot have faith in?' I felt the belief I had was too little for my experiences, and I was just lying there confused, and then I told the Lord certain things which I won't say now because they are a bit personal. I said all those things, and then this burning sensation went to the head, then back to my feet. And then the sensations gradually left the body. On getting up I found that I couldn't stand properly, and I staggered to my seat.

I heard the Lord's voice saying, 'Have you seen how much love I have for you?'

When I heard that, I was so moved. I don't know how many people were there, but I started crying. I cried, and cried, and cried. I hadn't known that the Lord would come down to earth and take actions of that nature. You see, I expected Him to do the big things, and we would have to cope with the little things ourselves. And here He was doing the three I didn't ask for. That was, honestly, one of the questions I asked.

I said, 'Lord, it's only my feet,' and He said, 'Well, I would do what you ask and even more – more than you need.'[1] That was one of the answers.

I got home, woke my husband up and told him the whole story before going to bed. All night the burning sensation was within the body, as if the healing was continuing. It went on and on through the night. The sinus kept dripping (I think it was so severe because I had had the problem since 1977), but there was no blockage, no pains, no sinus headaches. My hand sometimes used to feel paralyzed if I picked up something heavy like a glass of water: this was because of the sprained muscle in my chest. I haven't felt any such sensations since that day. My feet haven't swollen. Usually I couldn't possibly go off the medicines for three days before the legs would start swelling.

And I have been free ever since.

I decided to tell everybody the love of God. If He can do it for me, He can do it for anybody else.

More than two years since giving this testimony, Comfort is still free and rejoicing in what God did for her.

Comfort was not the only one to discover that God *is able to do exceeding abundantly above all that we ask or think* (Ephesians 3:20).

* * * * *

As I got out of my car to go into our bookshop one day near the end of 1996, I was met by **Mike** coming jauntily up Jamaica Street's steep brae, with an official-looking dossier under his arm. An ordinary encounter, you might say. But for anyone who knew Mike, it was rather extraordinary. As he says himself:

God loves to perform miracles, and I am one of them!
In 1986, when I was in my early forties, with a wife and two teenage sons to support, I had to retire on

medical grounds. In hospital it was confirmed that I had a muscular disorder in my right thigh which would worsen as I got older. Because the diameter of my thigh was starting to shrink, I had eventually to use a stick: it was the only way I could get about. Each year the pain in my leg got worse. My sleep was affected; there was very little I could do; the stairs of the tenement in which I live became difficult to negotiate.

'Lord, what about me? Why not touch me?' I cried one night as I listened over and over again to people giving testimony to healing.

The answer was unexpected. It came a week later during a Saturday night meeting in 1993. Mary was leading from the front, and the anointing that came through the singing was tremendous. While we were all standing, God spoke directly to me. He said, 'Embrace the pain.' Without fully understanding what it meant, I did it at the point when He spoke.

When the singing was finished and we sat down, the anointing of God increased on me, and suddenly I went prostrate in the pew where I was. Now if you could see that pew, you would realize that there is very little margin for error! The positioning must have been exact! I may say I have landed in some queer places. There was one time in the barn at our Wiston camp when everybody was falling round about me. When the anointing came on me I knew there was a space in front of me, but I would have to bend to get there. And that's what happened! When God hit me, He must have bent me: zap! That is typical of the anointing of God.

While I lay there in the pew, Jennifer Jack came over and ministered to me, and it was confirmed in my spirit that God did indeed want me to accept my condition along with the prospect of ending up in a wheelchair.[2] I think it was through my acceptance of the situation that God was free to work out His purposes in my life at that time.

To set this matter in perspective, it may be relevant to observe that Mike's Christian experience since his conversion at the age of seventeen had been at times erratic. Through his illness God was bringing a strong discipline to bear on his child. It is perhaps significant that by this time Mike was engaged in pioneering a new branch of our work. In this context it was extremely important that his own spiritual condition be one of deep dependence on God. There is a timing in the things of God, and it may also be that Mike had to wait for the coming of the 'new ministry' before he could receive the blessing that God had in store. Meanwhile, as he tells us:

> For the next three years the pain got worse. Every night became a nightmare: I hated going to bed, preferring to sit in an armchair. By this time not only my right leg but also my 'good' left leg was beginning to be affected.

Medically there was no hope of a cure. Then in November 1994 God moved in fresh power through the 'new ministry'. Mike describes his initial hesitation and what happened thereafter:

> I wasn't too sure about this movement at first. I had cautiously decided to sit back, and thought I would be the last person to go forward. But as people went up on to the platform and testified to what God had done in their lives when they went on to the carpet (or, as Mr Black describes it, the operating table of God), I listened and thought, 'Something is in that.'
> One Sunday night early in February 1995 I went to the meeting and prayed that Mrs Gault would offer ministry (there was no thought of healing in my mind). She did make the offer, and out I went.

As ministry was received, I was slain in the Spirit in the aisle, and the fire of God invaded my life. A sunburst of power came right through me. Lying there, I tried to get up on a few occasions but couldn't manage it. God hadn't finished working with me. Once He had finished, I was able to get up and walk back to my seat.

Now why I had left my stick in the pew I don't know. A registered nurse who was also on the carpet saw me cruising up the aisle, wondered where my stick was – and saw that there was no limp.[3]

That night I had a perfect night's sleep.

On the Monday morning, still unsure what had happened, I thought, 'I'll be very careful ... I'll wait and see.' Getting up in time for the prayer meeting at half-past-seven, I functioned all day with no walking stick. I thought, 'I'll still keep a low profile, just to be on the safe side.'

On the Tuesday morning, I went to our church in Skelmorlie to let in the glaziers (the little darlings down there had broken fourteen windows). For most of the morning I sanded down four tables we had recently acquired.

I went home in the afternoon, took the dog for a walk, and washed the car.

These are things that maybe seem not too significant – but to me they spelled a miracle! To do these things was a miracle!

That night, I threw away my orthopaedic pillow – 'Don't need you!'

By the Wednesday morning it had dawned on me, 'God is healing my life! There is no more pain in this good leg. There's a bit more strength coming in this bad leg.'

It was then that I went into the church bookshop and said to Mr Black and others, 'God has touched my life and He has healed me.' In His operating theatre – as I lay on the carpet – God had dealt with me. I hadn't come forward for healing; I had come forward for spiritual ministry. A miracle had been performed, and now I walked about with no limp at all.

I had spoken to Mike earlier about being healed. But no man or woman can heal. These things come by the power of the Spirit; they are not in our hand. When the miracle took place the effect on people who had known Mike through the years was profound. An awe fell over the bookshop that day. Mike was walking – after eight years. Glory be to God! While slight vestiges of pain still remained, something of great significance had occurred.

Mike's summing up of the situation at that point was this:

> Anything can happen when God moves – and He is moving in these days. I am glad today to be able to say I am being healed. I am not yet fully healed; at the moment there is still a pain in the thigh. But, praise God, that will go as well. I feel as though He has taken away all the inflammation of this wound, and eventually it will heal. I am glad to be able to testify, and for Mr Black to see the spiritual son who has given so much bother over all the years eventually being free from eight years of agony! Blessed be God's holy Name!

For about a year and a half Mike continued to function freely, although the healing was not yet complete. Then the bombshell occurred: the pain returned.

> I was particularly upset about this. Why would God heal me, and then allow the pain to come back? Unable to understand why this had happened, I spoke to both Mr Black and Mrs Gault. Was my life after all to end in a wheel-chair? Going home afterwards, I went before God.

Both Grace and I were considerably disturbed at this unforeseen turn of events. But we soon felt very strongly that Mike should resist the return of illness. Grace had not forgotten the power with which God had come upon Mike that night in the aisle of the Greenock church.

It was at this juncture that there occurred one of those 'coincidences' in which one senses God's guiding hand. Grace had recently acquired a substantial book on the American preacher John G. Lake. Hoping to find something that would speak to Mike's situation, she opened it to find herself in the same moment reading about a remarkably similar case. Lake's own son had known a miraculous healing followed by the resurgence of his illness. Not until the father went to the bedside and persisted in prayer with his son was the healing restored. On reading this, Grace immediately passed the book to Mike for his encouragement.

Mike takes up the story:

> Soon afterwards at a Saturday night meeting in Glasgow Mr Black offered ministry to any whose pain had returned after they had been healed. When I went forward, Grace and Diana took me aside and prayed with me; then they asked me to come into the vestry for further ministry.
>
> That night a spirit of violence was discerned. This had been present from the time before I became a Christian, and I was fully delivered from it the same night. It had been there all these years: a foothold for the devil to get in and disrupt my life and bring back the disease in my leg. With the deliverance, healing returned to my body, and I became as strong as I am now. Praise be to God!

God was to do even more for Mike. His sickness benefit was due to end, and (in common with many others in the Greenock area) he had no prospect of employment. He continues:

My wife spoke to me about her feeling that she should go into the church coffee/bookshop full time. She knew that this would mean less money coming into the house. But she put it before God, and He said, 'Do it.' When she spoke to Ian Lundie (who is head of the catering staff), he said, 'That is an answer to prayer.'

Coming back home Jean felt good about it. Then suddenly the devil came in and said, 'You are a fool! Do you realize what you've done? You are going to have less money!'

She thought, 'What am I going to do?'

Turning to a small book (which Mike noted was 'supposed to be for daily readings – but my wife uses it at any page at all!') she read under the heading of 'Gracious Uncertainty':

> *The nature of the spiritual life is that we are certain in our uncertainty.*
>
> *We are uncertain of our next step, but we are certain of God.*

The writer was Oswald Chambers, commenting on the verse, *It has not yet been revealed what we shall be* (1 John 3:2).[4] Opening another page, Jean read under the heading 'The Concept of Divine Control' the following verse and comment,

> *How much more will your Father who is in heaven give good things to those who ask Him!*   (Matthew 7:11)

> *Jesus urges us to keep our minds filled with the concept of God's control over everything, which means that a disciple must maintain an attitude of perfect trust and an eagerness to ask and to seek.*
>
> *Not even the smallest detail of life happens unless God's will is behind it.*

60

That, according to Mike, was enough proof for Jean that she was making the right decision. He describes what happened next:

> She woke me up one morning, saying, 'Come into the kitchen while I eat my breakfast. I want to speak to you.'
>
> 'Have I done something wrong about the house?' I wondered. 'Have I not done the polishing, or something...?' Since my wife had become wage earner for the family, I did the housework.
>
> 'What is it?' I asked.
>
> 'God has spoken to me, and He has asked for you to take over my job.' Jean was a financial agent who collected from door to door.
>
> I did not give her a complete answer right away; I studied it for a moment or two. Then I realized that God was in this. I said, 'Fair enough. Go for it, girl. Put it to your boss and see what happens.'
>
> Her bosses thought it was a wonderful idea, and had no difficulty securing the agreement of the area manager.

When he gave this testimony in the church where he had received his healing, Mike summed up his situation in these words:

> This man standing here is now in full employment! You see how God moves: it is wonderful! Not only has He healed my body; He has given me a job also. Who wants a fifty-three-year-old man? God is in control, hallelujah! Blessed be His wonderful Name.

Considering that Greenock has one of the highest unemployment rates in the country, it was wonderful that Mike should walk effortlessly, both literally and metaphorically, into a job! Mike is – in common with many others – a living evidence of the truth of Christ's promise:

> *But seek ye first the kingdom of God, and his right-*
> *eousness; and all these things shall be added unto you.*
> (Matthew 6:33 AV)

Notes

[1] Comfort had strongly in mind the verse *Now unto Him that is able to do exceeding abundantly above all that we ask or think . . .* (Ephesians 3:20). Two years later, she affirms that the words spoken to her by Christ continue to be wonderfully fulfilled.

[2] Jennifer Jack is in charge of our church in Falkirk. Her testimony appears in my *Consider Him: The Qualities of Christ* (New Dawn Books, 1988).

[3] The registered nurse was Isabel Hardie, whose testimony appears later in the trilogy. The aisle of which Mike speaks is a sloping one, so that before his healing it would have been easier for him to move down to the front than to walk back up without his stick.

[4] The book was the pocket-sized, condensed version of Oswald Chambers' *My Utmost for His Highest* published by Christian Art, 1994 (originally published by Discovery House Publications, 1992; © Oswald Chambers Publications). The readings quoted are for 29 April and 16 July respectively.

Chapter 5

To Work, to War

The student comes in waving a certificate.

'Well, Dad, there is the degree, there is the evidence that I've made the grade. I'm going to put my feet up now and sit idle here for evermore.'

Had one of mine ever ventured such a suggestion, I would have said, 'Well, my child, you may sit idle, but you won't sit idle here! Your degree opens the door to a whole new life. You are not at an end; you are at a beginning. Your time to work has come!'

There were many who went into a new dimension of God-consciousness under the new ministry. They may not have attended services with any deliberate intention of experiencing this, any more than on many another occasion. But the Lord was there and reached them where they sat. Their feet brought them to the front, the power of God put them on their backs, and many went through into another world. There was healing, there was miracle, and they were on the operating table of God – and that happened too to some who never left their seats. And what happened in our company has happened to many across the world.

I have a word for such people. You are not called of God merely to enjoy one glorious moment of lying on a beautiful carpet. You are not called for one exclusive experience. You are taken into another dimension to live in there always – not to come back out through that door, but to live there and know the joy and the power and the glory of that dimension, and to carry it and emanate it so that other lives may be caught in the blazing fire that comes from your life. I am not saying that doorway is only found by lying on the floor. You may enter that dimension on your two feet, or where you sit in your seat. But the vital point is that you go into that place and know God in there, that God may work through you in all your paths of life.

There were some of our company who did not need me to tell them these things. Often it was the pressure of outward circumstances that brought them to the place where they heard Christ's voice for themselves. One was **Isobel**, a nurse whose first experience of the new ministry was immediately tested by an uncommonly stressful week on the ward. In her own words:

Sitting in the congregation I wanted to go forward for prayer. But when the moment came I froze in my seat, unable to walk out to the front. Most of the church had emptied before I plucked up courage to ask Mr Black to pray with me.

There was a strong sense of control the whole time the Holy Spirit was on me, and I was very much aware of choice to go with Him. I found myself going down and lying there thinking, 'I'm lying on the ground!' Then the Holy Spirit fell, covering my whole body. The sense of the presence of God was all around me. I was aware that I was lying in a church and that the presence of God was heavy upon me. I was aware of the Holy Spirit being there, and of His character and very nature. And I just lay, not wanting to move.

'Is it time to get up?' I wondered.

No, it wasn't time to get up; it was time to stay there and to soak in the presence of God.

Immediately afterwards I had the most horrendous week at work. I slept in twice! And I found by midweek I was really ruffled inside. My mind was aching with over-activity. Praying for mental control, I found that Jesus said, 'Go into My presence. Go into that depth of My presence.' And as I did so, I found that tremendous peace and the sense of God with me again. But before Friday (I said it was a horrendous week!) I was beginning to feel condemned because I had failed to maintain that place that God had given me. And I thought, well, He really didn't want me to live in it all the time. It couldn't possibly be for **me** to stay in that place.

But the presence of Christ in the next weekend meeting was just beautiful with the sense of His gentleness, His loveliness and His sweetness. He spoke quite clearly to me and said, 'No, Isobel, this is for you and this is the place you're to be in all the time. This **is** yours, it's been won for you, this is yours!'

There is a sense of wonder at the marvellous things God has for us.

Isobel valued her experience of this new depth of Christ sufficiently to want it to permeate her work situation. Perhaps not every week was as stressful as the one she describes. Yet job-stress is something of which we hear a great deal these days. In particular, there are many who are feeling the effects as the winds of change blow through the professions at every level.

For months **Eric**, employed by a well-known supermarket chain, had been dismayed by some of the changes in management style that had been imposed in a particularly draconian manner in his own store. Hurt and indeed angered at the treatment of many of his colleagues, he felt that there were strong 'New Age' overtones in the philosophy behind these changes. It took him a little longer to realize that there was also a deep problem in himself. When he did realize this, with characteristic vigour he set about changing his reactions. To do this, and to find a way of coping with the situation at work, he needed a miracle. He told his story a few weeks later:

The first time I received ministry I had been very much under assault at work. When I was prayed for by Ruth, I had a wonderful vision, but I did not go down, and indeed I did not feel God.[1] In that vision I felt I was led into the courts of heaven by Christ on one side and the Holy Spirit on the other, and I still did not feel a thing. I wasn't able to experience it emotionally, although I could see it very clearly before my eyes. There was a blockage: and I was aware of what it was.

I had been having a great deal of hassle at work, and indeed a very nasty situation had arisen for us all. The problem was one of management style. The store in which I work was very old-fashioned. We didn't conform to all the company's new techniques of getting the most out of people; many of my colleagues were dismissed and we were all under pressure.

The new techniques we were urged to adopt were based very much on what I believed were New Age philosophies. I don't know very much about New Age, but I've recognized in the past year or so an incredibly dark move that way.

There were all sorts of problems. For example, I was given a poster to put up in my office, headed 'Ten Rules of the Demon'. I read it, and found it dreadful. It was the opposite of the ten commandments! Its advice was (in a nutshell): 'Hate one another, fight with one another, contradict one another, and you will all grow into very strong, wonderful people.' So I took mine down and I put up the ten commandments! Which I thought was very funny – but the very same day I was severely reprimanded for it and told to put the other one back up (which I never did, though I took the ten commandments down). There were real, strong forces against me, and it actually wasn't funny at all.

I had watched my friends either getting sacked or resigning. The pressure applied on the management team in my store was incredible. Many of those affected were friends that in spiritual places I had fought hard for. They were really good friends, they knew where I stood, and they were very open to the gospel. Not only did I feel that those who came in and chased them away were bringing dark forces with them, causing me real disappointment because I had fought hard for that place; but, worse, I found myself hating the people who did this. Three or four of my very closest friends had been sacked, and another couple of them had gone. It is just dreadful what they are doing to my friends who are still in the store. On a natural level it is really easy to hate people who are doing that to your friends. I found that people were coming up and asking me, 'What can we do to sort this out?' I seemed to be the centre of all the militance in the store. And basically I let hatred in.

It suddenly occurred to me, 'O Lord, this isn't me. I love people; I love souls. These people are lost; I love people. How am I able to say these things about them?' And a real war started in my life over all of this. I have known God often put unsaved people on my heart, and I'll cry for hours. I'll go to outreach meetings and if somebody is saved I'll rejoice for a time, and then I'll think of all the ones that didn't get saved and I'll cry; I can spend a whole night in tears. And I suddenly found that I didn't love these people – these were unsaved, and I didn't love them! I positively hated them.

The situation had still not been resolved when Eric went for further ministry at the end of the day on which he had already received prayer.

This time I found myself on the floor, as Alison Speirs prayed with me.[2] Everything comes in pictures to me, and almost immediately I had another vision. I was trapped at the bottom of the ocean, with reeds all around me. Although I wasn't struggling for breath, I knew that I was going to drown, for I didn't know how to get up. I was not fighting, but just lying there, and hope was draining out of me.

And from a great height it must have come: breaking through the surface of the water and plunging down near where I lay, came the cross of Christ. As it plunged down, I saw it coming. It slowed and ultimately stopped – and I thought, 'That's going to vanish if I don't move quickly!' And so I grasped it and held on to it. Breaking all the reeds as I clung on to it, it took me up to the surface, where I lay with it beside me. This must have taken only a couple of seconds after Alison had prayed with me. When I came to again, my hands were holding on for all I was worth – to nothing!

I said, 'O God, what are you saying to me?'

And I felt very clearly that I was to hold on to the cross, and the cross at this point was very much involved in the work situation. I was to find the place of love for these people. I went back to my work after that, very encouraged, because I had broken through; God had touched me emotionally. It wasn't like the earlier type of vision, where I had seen wonderful things but could not enter into them. Now God had broken through.

For the first week back at work I was very pleased with what went on, because, although I can't say I loved these people, God held me so that I wasn't saying things against them – which was an incredible, God-given victory for me at the time.

A few weeks have passed since, and things have moved on again. It's still a dreadfully hard sort of thing to bear at times, but God has shown me love for the people and hate for what seems to be behind it. I think the New Age philosophy is very much there – and that God has held me.

There follows a typically 'Eric' touch. Accustomed to attracting a great deal of comment for his Christian beliefs, he was intrigued to see that the newcomers seemed oblivious to the fact. He did not, however, attempt to take refuge in what might have seemed welcome obscurity to someone in his situation:

> When Satan moves against me I always like to do something back. He once woke me up with a nightmare, and so I wrote a gospel letter and sent it to all my family. He's never done it again (I've never had another nightmare)! I feel that when the devil is pushing forward on something, then there is always a chance for us to gain ground.
>
> And so, just after all this has happened, I have written a letter applying for permission to hold an open-air meeting right outside the store. It is my desire that things will backfire on the devil for what he is doing in that place.

I believe that many of us are meeting the same forces in our places of work that Eric met. Some are much more subtly disguised than they seemed to be in Eric's situation, where they were very overt. But these forces are real, and as a church we prayed that Eric would be strengthened to stand against the powers of darkness.

One day many months later we asked Eric how things were going with himself and his job. It transpired that they were going very well indeed. The open-air meeting had been allowed to run and had borne fruit; and a new management with a more humane approach had been installed in his place of work.

I have an instinctive sympathy for Eric's refusal to leave all the initiative with the enemy. One of the hymns that

God gave us around that time was 'The Song of War', which I read to the company, commenting as I went:

> The winds of God are blowing,
>   Blowing everywhere;
> The words of God are sounding,
>   Sounding on the air.
> Prepare the ground for battle,
>   For God's day has come:
> Drive back the powers of darkness,
>   And march to sounding drum.

There is knowledge in the land that a new wind is blowing. Men and women of God are persuaded that while there may be excesses and mistakes, there is a wind that blows from heaven, and we must not miss that blowing wind.

As yet, in many places the unsaved are not pouring in. Up to this present point in our own areas it is largely Christians who are being affected, but not the masses of the unsaved. And the heart of Christ is ever longing over Jerusalem, a-weeping for the sins of Jerusalem, a-weeping for the people.

But God's day has come. Get the beat of the drum in your blood, and the drive of God in your soul! Up, gird on your swords! Now is the time for battle – wonderful, glorious battle – and the opportunity it affords.

> Long years the land lay shrouded,
>   Shrouded in defeat:
> There was the breath of evil,
>   There was Satan's seat.
> But now the winds are blowing,
>   And darkness flees the plain:
> The power of God is flowing,
>   And many are the slain.

Surely we knew the breath of evil. But, oh, the flowing

of the power of God! Far, far greater than all the powers of evil. He will overturn, and overturn; He will change the face of the nation: I believe it absolutely. Hell will be driven back before the coming onslaught of the power of God.

> Hark to the sounding trumpet,
>   Hark to the blaring horn!
> Now is the day of battle
>   When many shall be born.
> Sing now the song of Zion,
>   Sing loud the swelling praise;
> Sing of the glorious Lion,
>   And loud the anthems raise.

When the first part of this verse came, I wondered – and then I said, 'Yes, I love these words: **blaring horn**! The harsh note of war! Not a soft **Tootery-tootery-toot**, but the horn of war.

> Praise Him, praise Him, Lord of Glory,
>   Praise Him, praise Him, Lord of Life.
> See He rides in triumph,
>   Victorious in the strife.

> Crown Him Lord of glory,
>   Crown Him Lord of life.
> See the Lord of battles
>   Victorious in the strife.

Yes, war is wonderful – when we are on the side of the angels, or when the angels are on our side. But we must always remember that

> *our struggle is not against flesh and blood, but against the rulers, against the authorities, against the powers of this dark world and against the spiritual forces of evil in the heavenly realms.*   (Ephesians 6:12–13)

71

We must be in the right condition to engage in our warfare successfully. Israel discovered this when she was defeated at Ai because of sin in the camp, and Achan had to be exposed and dealt with. So do our Achans in our day. Eric had to have hatred turned to love before victory was his.

> *For though we live in the world, we do not wage war as the world does. The weapons we fight with are not the weapons of the world. On the contrary, they have divine power to demolish strongholds.*
>
> (2 Corinthians 10:3−4)

When we are right with God we may advance to victory.

Notes

[1] Ruth Gollan is in charge of a group whose activities are centred mainly in the Johnstone and Kilbarchan areas of Renfrewshire, with a strong focus on children's work.

[2] Alison Speirs (who wrote the foreword to this book), plays a leading part in church activities in Greenock and Glasgow. Her testimony appears in chapter 8 below. Her life story is found in my book *Revival: Personal Encounters* (New Dawn Books, 1993), Part 2.

Chapter 6

Cleaning the Tiles

As God dealt with the blockage in Eric's life, so He probed out areas of spiritual or moral weakness in other lives that submitted to His touch. Although there was nothing harsh in His treatment, sin was brought to the surface and effectively cleansed and subdued by the Spirit's power.

We have seen how He did it for Eric in the last chapter. He did it for another young man, now much used of God. There was in **Andrew**'s inner being an impassable barrier, a serious blockage that had to be removed. One night God brought it sharply to his attention:

> I must have lain in bed for a couple of hours in the presence of God, feeling Him stirring up things that had troubled me. Some of the things are too private to speak about, but one main thing was the area of untruthfulness.
>
> When I was at school I had got myself into a situation where I began to lie to people there and also to my family at home. It got to the stage where lying almost became a part of me. Even after I came back to Christ and really gave myself to Him and made deep decisions to follow Him, when the light of God would come to me there was always this area that couldn't totally endure the clear shining of the light of God.

Then one night at a meeting, during the time of singing before the preaching had even started, he felt God come on him:

> He showed me my life in the form of an iron bar. And there was a twist in it, as if the devil had got hold of a big hammer and given it a good crack. I had tried and tried and prayed and prayed to God to give me victory on the relevant issues, but try as I might I couldn't do anything to reverse this twist. I remember one night about a year ago going home and deciding that I was just going to go before God until I got victory on it, and I wasn't going to move. I remember going up to my room and lying on the floor, and crying out to God, 'Lord, give me victory on this.' I don't know how much later it was that I got up – and I still didn't have victory on it.
>
> But on this more recent occasion I went forward for prayer, and I felt God really started to do something in me. I said to Miss (Mary) Black at the end, 'I don't feel as if it's complete yet. There are things that I think God is speaking to me about.' I told her about the iron bar.
>
> On the Sunday night in our young folks' prayer meeting (where God moves week after week on us), Mrs Gault came over and prayed with me, and in an instant I was down on the floor. I felt a light come almost immediately. It didn't gradually get brighter; it was as if God was suddenly there, and bits of me opened right up to God that I hadn't had the power to open, though I'd tried. God Himself opened them up and His light came in. I suddenly felt a pain from deep down inside that I hadn't even known was there – it came right up and out into the light of God. Almost as suddenly as it had come, it left, and the prayer meeting ended. I felt as if I was a new person. I didn't know exactly what had happened, but the next day when I got up I felt totally different. God had

actually changed part of my nature and managed to remake that iron bar that had been so bent. I hadn't really believed that God could ever do that. In theory I knew He could, but I had thought, 'I'm going to have to live with this. I'm going to have to fight this till I die – I'm just going to have to take it with me to the grave.' And in an instant of time God took it away.

Now I can feel myself starting to make lists – you know, 'Well, if God can change that, He can change this, and He can change this . . . !'

It has opened a new place in God to me, a new place of freedom. In another meeting God came really close, and (this ties up with what other people have said) it was as if there was a light and a place in God where I could lose myself and get right out into Him. It just brushed against me for two seconds, so to speak. But that is where I am going. Anything that God speaks to me about I believe He can take away; He can change any of us and bring us right into that pure light where we are not conscious of ourselves, but right out in God.

In a moment of time a whole inner being can be changed radically by the action of God. It has caused wonderment through the years how those who come into our midst with phobias are healed so drastically, so quickly and so permanently. But that, to me, is a small matter, compared to the kind of thing of which Andrew speaks: of that innerness of being suddenly gripped by the Holy Spirit and in a moment of time turned round, straightened out, brought back on to the level.

Barriers between Himself and His church are intolerable to God. As I pondered this in relation to what was happening among our people, one picture recurred again and again. The memory comes from my early days on a farm. The farm had ground of various kinds. There was one stretch which was quite low-lying, and it produced reeds and rushes if not drained. Occasionally parts of it would be under water and the drains got clogged. Picture a winter morning. The drains were opened up, and you took the hollow tiles up from the bottom and laid them along the side. In frosty weather they were very cold, and the sludge that was inside had hardened. It was your job to take each tile individually and bump it on a stone or whatever was available, to dislodge the sludge – whether it was frozen or by that time thawed. It was a dirty job, it was a cold job, it was quite frankly a horrible job.

What were we doing? We were cleaning the sludge out of the tile, so that when that tile was put back in place the flow of the water through it would be unimpeded. There would be no blockage, there would be nothing to prevent a free flow.

You may look at your life and the lives of men and women as channels (tiles in the farming language, but channels is a word with which you are likely to be more familiar). The channel can be clogged, and the water of God can be impeded in its flow because the channel is blocked. God comes to carry out an operation which will cause the clogging, the things that are causing the hindrance, to be taken away. And here we realized the exceeding love of God. He came as the good physician, the kind, the gentle, the loving God. When we dealt with the drain, we had to pick up every individual tile. It was not something we could deal with en masse; we handled every tile. So in our times of ministry He came into our midst to take up every individual tile and give it a little knock, to get out of it everything that should not be there.

So it was with **Margaret**, whose miraculous healing from ME has been described in an earlier publication.[1] Her account of God's dealing with her a few years later shows very clearly the stage-by-stage progress of the divine operation and human co-operation. The very night that the new wave of the Spirit began in Greenock Margaret, without being present, was nevertheless affected:

The Holy Spirit began dealing in my life at the very start of this move of God. Strangely, I felt its effects even though unable to be at the meeting on that first Saturday night. Conviction of sin came strongly on me in relation to faults that I had not recognized as 'important' or gross sins. On my return to Glasgow I came to the Sunday night meeting, and again I felt the glory of God come down upon me.

While Mr Black was ministering at the front and people were receiving the anointing and being touched of God, I did not feel any direction of the Spirit to go forward. But His power came upon me nevertheless, convicting of sin, so that I couldn't lift my head. One issue was that of angry reactions, not shown outwardly but nursed inwardly against people and circumstances. God strongly convicted me of it all, and I gave over the sins as far as I could, confessing them to God, seeking His cleansing and help.

It was a changed person that left the meeting that night. Throughout that week I was very careful with other people in my thoughts, actions, and words – especially at work, where I felt God wanted me to be a clear witness and to take a stronger stand in purity and in the righteousness of God. Without joining in the things of sin I hadn't wanted to be unpopular, and I knew that taking a firmer line would not be easy. But God was with me.

Towards the Friday night in Glasgow I knew the Holy Spirit was going to touch me. When the call was given to go forward, the Spirit clearly showed that I was to go and receive His touch. Before Mr Black even came I felt the power of God coming on me and my body beginning to weaken physically, but the spirit beginning to live and to rise towards God. With the anointing there was a burst of light, and as I lay prostrate in the hands of the Holy Spirit God began to deal with me.

During the first part of the experience the Holy Spirit was falling on me like a heavy weight, and I had no choice but to lie there. I couldn't have got up if I'd tried; I couldn't move at all. The Spirit began to deal again with the wrong reactions and the sin in my life, clearing it all out, delivering me from it and cleansing me inside. That went on for quite a while. I must say, although it's like deliverance and cleansing, it was a pleasant experience. I was in the hands of the Holy Spirit. I didn't even feel the hardness of the floor; it was as if I was held by the Spirit on cushions or clouds. It was a pleasant, happy experience, and the gentleness of Christ was there.

In the next stage it seemed that I was being lifted up in my spirit away from my body, higher and higher into the realms of God. That is what I had desired: I had been longing for it for a long, long time, perhaps for years: just to be lifted up into a higher dimension, where the things of the Spirit, the things of Christ, are very real, not just remote things and not felt only when one is joining in with others or relying on someone else. I had been seeking that blessing and that lifting up into the higher realms and had asked God to take me there. And so I lay in the hands of the Spirit, prostrate for quite some time. I knew when it was over. But the weight of the Spirit was still upon me so that it was difficult to get up off the floor.

After that I felt the presence of Christ in my house much more strongly. The next morning I was up very early just worshipping Christ. I simply wanted to spend time with Him, to praise and worship Him, even if quietly: there didn't have to be noise. I sat in the silence with God, letting the experience deepen in my life. It has definitely changed me. I am far more conscious of sin, guarding against temptation and the reactions that can come when situations or people cause hurt. God was saying, 'It's your reactions I'm looking at, not what the people are doing to you.' But

I praise God that I did not miss such a lovely experience: feeling the love of Christ and the gentleness around me, and the changes He has brought in my life.

I have not met anybody yet who has come on to God's operating table in this way who has not rejoiced in the afterward. An illustration often comes back to me. Have you ever been damp, wet, cold, and shivering and gone into your home to find that the water has been heated, and you have slipped into a hot bath? You are not in a hurry, and there is nobody else going to be knocking on the door and saying, 'Hurry up, I want in there!' The family are all out, and you've got the house to yourself. You have endless time, and you luxuriate in the glorious warmth. You bathe in it. Memory is a strange thing. I remember one bath I had more than any other bath in all my life.

The bath was the consequence of motoring down to England to take meetings. It was extremely bad weather, and I was due there on a Saturday. I left on the Friday night, knowing that the roads were unusually dangerous. As I was going towards Abington on my way to the Border I noticed that diesel lorries were abandoned at the side of the road; their fuel had frozen and they could go no further. I was young in these days, and it was a kind of farming tradition that you very seldom if ever turned back: it wasn't the done thing. You put your hand to the plough and you went ahead. Was it raining? That was tough. Was it snowing? Well, it was snowing. Was it freezing? Then it was freezing. But that night it got real bad, I may tell you. The roads were fearful, and I was frozen.

So I decided that when I got to Abington I might as well stay the night and travel on in the morning – only to find that there were no beds in Abington and I couldn't stay the night. I was advised that the nearest place was Gretna. So on I went down to Gretna. The accommodation was purpose-built wooden chalets; they were most comfortable. It was wonderful getting in, freezing cold, to a lovely warm room, with a bathroom en suite, hot water, and the best bath I think I ever had in all my life!

Going on to God's operating table is like a cold man going into a wonderful bath. He will take nothing away that you will ultimately want to retain. He will give you what your soul needs, as He did for Margaret – and then, a few weeks later, for **Pat**, one of our workers with an evangelistic gift.

Pat came to me one day in our book shop, obviously much moved. She knew that it was right to be involved in what was happening on a Saturday night, but she hadn't 'got in'. I listened to the problems that she outlined, and I did not feel like preaching her a sermon. I just said, 'Listen, Pat, you will go into the arms of Jesus, and He'll touch all of these things that you have spoken about. He'll deal with them all. He loves you. Just go into the arms of Jesus. But there's no need to wait for a Saturday night.' I think it gave Pat quite a shock; she probably was not thinking of immediate ministry. I said, 'I'll stand behind you. I'll not put you down – but if you go down you'll be all right.' And sure enough, down she went.

I remained with her for a short time and spoke to her a bit. Then I saw her hands going up and a smile coming across her face. Glory be to God! So I went out and shut the door. Do you know, it was about two or three hours afterwards that I suddenly remembered I had left her lying there! I hoped she would be all right; and then I had a picture of somebody maybe coming in and thinking there was a dead body lying up at the back, because I had told nobody what was happening! But in due course she emerged to tell her own story:

My problem was hurts, some of which I had held on to for four or five years. I appreciated very much what someone else had said about hurts that wouldn't go away, because I too couldn't cope with them. The odd thing was that I never felt I could go to God with them; I was hurting so much. What I didn't like about the situation was that it was changing me. I was becoming a very horrible person. In building up a defence, I was, in my own language, pig-ignorant to people. I just wasn't going to let them trample over me in any way: I had had enough.

But I began to see how ridiculous this was – because I knew the way God was moving in our Saturday night meeting, and I was scared out my wits that I would miss what God was doing because of what I was holding on to. So I came to Mr Black. Later on I discovered that he was particularly busy, but at the time he gave no indication of being in a hurry.

He simply said, 'You're lucky to get me, because I was nearly away.'

I was glad of that, because I had made up my mind to speak to him about my problem even though it nearly killed me! And I am more than glad of it now – because what happened afterwards was just as Mr Black said. I don't think you could put into words what you feel in that time. I will say one thing. I had peace in my soul that I haven't had in years – and this I appreciate tremendously.

Not only had peace been lacking: it had been many a year since I laughed. But on that same evening in our Port Glasgow meeting as God continued to work on me He brought me into a place of laughter. God is so gracious, and I praise His holy Name.

You should be very free, if God gives you laughter. There is no place for strained human laughter, but if God gives it, be sure not to miss it! Pat was one of many to experience joy and satisfaction as they yielded to God and allowed Him to operate on their lives.

It is worth commenting further on one of the problems that has surfaced so far in various testimonies in this book. It is the problem of wrong reactions. As I had occasion to know, these can take very subtle forms. The following incident occurred only a short time before I ministered to Pat.

After a time of deep blessing, I had found myself quite irritated. An issue had arisen between myself and one of my daughters. You realize I was right, of course! But she thought she was right. She can be quite stubborn (you know how girls often take after their mothers!). So we fought it out for quite a long time, and she was adamant, I was adamant. I found, however, that my spiritual life was dented a bit – but it was not too deeply disturbed, and I had quite a good night.

There came the morning, and I thought, 'I'll just put one small point to her that I maybe haven't emphasized sufficiently.' We were on our way to a funeral, and I put this point most reasonably, and she put something back, and so I had to reply – and before you knew where you were, we were arguing again! Not for a moment did I think I was wrong in what I was saying or doing, and probably neither did she.

But we both realized that there was a funeral coming up, where our being in good form could be very significant for many people, and I think we both just denied ourselves and died to the matter, and opened to God. Suddenly I found a barrier that I hadn't realized was there. Now I did not at any point do anything I thought was wrong. But I had allowed reactions that seemed perfectly reasonable to rise in me, and without realizing it I lost the sharpness of the sense of the presence of God. And let's just put it in honest words: the devil had got a foothold. I wasn't pursuing something intentionally evil, you understand. I was being honest with myself. But I was allowing human reactions to rise. They were perfectly understandable, but they were putting the sharp edge of the presence of God at a distance. I repented deeply. But it was quite a time before I got back to where I had been. The devil had got a foothold.

We may learn from this. The devil does not always need a gross temptation with which to tempt you – nor even a pleasant, carnal temptation. He can get you irritated on something about which you feel fully justified. But you are not noticing that in going down that road you are at that very moment losing the sweetness of the presence of Christ. Friends, I can't afford to be without the depth of that presence. There are issues and people to be dealt with constantly, and I need to know God. I need that mighty anointing of God. I need to know Him, and so do you. Nothing is to be allowed to replace the presence of God. Think of Solomon's temple, full of the glory of God's presence. Can you imagine some of the priests, waiting on the outskirts to minister but unable while that power and glory was there, being all concerned with natural things and injustices that had happened to them, feeling sorry for themselves because of someone who was going a different way? Nothing should flow through you but the presence and the power of God. You are not allowed to let anything replace God. You have to die to it. I had to die to it, put it right out, totally out, that the fullness of the presence of Christ might come back.

Are you dwelling in that fullness of presence, without a ripple, without a feeling of injustice, without anything of self rising to the surface? We must put off the old self, that the new creature might be manifest. God is a good God, a forgiving God, a loving God. And God forgives us, even when we have not felt guilty. We may suddenly know we have been at fault although we did not feel so at the time. We may have felt fully justified but God judged us guilty, for all that. 'You have allowed My presence to be disturbed in the innerness of your being, and that is sin.' You were right, perchance – but you were wrong. You shouldn't have let the irritation get in to the point it did. You should never have let it touch that sweet, gracious, wonderful presence of God. I love that presence.

God forgave me and restored my soul. You don't wait for a week to get restored. The moment you know there is something wrong, get it right immediately; don't fight with it. I found that it was tough: when the devil gets in, he doesn't get out quite so easily. He tries to hang on, and you have to wait for the action of God finally to put him out where he can't touch you, can't scratch you any more.

It was to make His presence our dwelling place, and to make our lives His dwelling place, that God came to cleanse and make whole. He came to those who already knew Him and loved Him. Those who experienced His dealing with sin could testify that it was always covered by His love.

Note

[1] In my *Christ the Deliverer* (New Dawn Books, 1991), chapter 6.

Chapter 7

Within the Veil

'Dear Old Boss' (the letter began),

First of all I want to let you know that you were right again ... but this time I am utterly thrilled that I have been wrong – and that is a turn-up for the books!

The letter had arrived early one Monday morning in January. The reference to 'Old Boss' recalled the days when I was a headmaster and **Irene** was first my pupil and then a member of my staff. She was also a particularly active member of my congregation. That she should have finished and handed in her letter with such despatch en route to her job in the middle of a busy teaching term was entirely typical of the energy with which she approached every aspect of her life.

Irene had struggled at first with the question of what should be her response to the new ministry. Finally one Friday night towards the end of January she indicated her desire for it, and received what she felt was only part of what God had for her. Some confusion which she does not specify arose on the Saturday, but she managed to put it aside and find the current of God's will for her on the Sunday night.

The letter continued:

> Thank you for your kindness on Friday which helped
> me break through part of my self-consciousness in
> moving out towards Christ. I felt the deep awe of
> which you spoke but, as I explained on Saturday
> morning, I didn't feel the thing was complete and so I
> was out on a sort of limb throughout that day. You
> know about Saturday night. [X-----]'s kindness really
> helped me not to go down. I think I realised that here
> was an opportunity to apply the teaching of death to
> human reactions, and if I did so something good
> could come out of something very confusing.
>
> But what about tonight [Sunday]? Unexpectedly,
> from my point of view, Grace felt led to invite people
> to come forward for ministry, and I felt the urge of
> the Spirit to raise my hand (without a struggle) ...
> and to go forward (with only a momentary qualm).
> There was absolutely no stress or tension even as I
> waited to receive ministry, and when Grace called me
> over and began to pray I felt myself sinking effort-
> lessly into deep heaven. No trauma about rocking on
> heels – I just seemed to glide down (maybe slipped –
> but it felt like gliding).
>
> Again, what you say about that carpet is totally
> accurate. It was the most desirable place in all the
> world to me then because as I lay there I felt
> enwrapped in peace. Christ came to me and revealed
> His beauty and His love in a deeper way than I could
> ever have imagined. I found Him although I didn't
> think I had lost Him! There was not a hint of
> reproach in His coming but rather a sense of being
> welcomed and wanted unreservedly. Imagine the joy
> that broke deep in me when Grace said He wasn't
> angry with me, but had been waiting for me to come.
>
> I can't put into words the sequence of events after
> that. There was a revelation of beauty – harmony and
> wholeness represented visually by a fragrant garden.

There was a sense of weightlessness and timelessness –
'the silence of eternity interpreted by love'.[1] As I lay
there drinking this in I realised that I was more
relaxed in that atmosphere than I'd ever been before.
It was my home; I know it because I've been there
before. It links with an atmosphere that often comes
down upon us towards the close of meetings but
which seems transitory and very vulnerable to dissipa-
tion. But it wasn't vulnerable or ethereal tonight. It
was strong, constant and unassailable. It was the real
world, and no jarring, discordant chords could
destroy the harmonious melody which pervaded its
atmosphere – music, colour, smell all vibrantly real
but not in a way that I could put into words.

I lay and basked in this beauty, and when I
eventually got up I was drunk with the joy of it.
I have not felt as happy or whole as this in years.
Indeed, I was reminded of my Baptism [in the Spirit]
when I came out of the vestry feeling that I had been
'filled with new wine'. Tonight the New Year Word
[1995] has taken on a new preciousness for me – 'This
is my rest forever. Here will I dwell. For the Lord has
chosen Irene, He has desired her for His habita-
tion ...'[2] I'm thrilled and overwhelmed and I thought
Old Boss would like to know and maybe he would
like to rejoice with me. I hope you can catch the joy in
the atmosphere.

Irene

'There speaks a soul in touch with God,' I commented
after reading this letter out for the encouragement of the
congregation in Glasgow the following week. Asked then
to supplement her account, Irene observed:

There is very little to add to that. It sums up what I
experienced last week. Obviously when you have
written to someone who was your old boss in the
secular world, it is quite embarrassing when it is read

out in as much detail as that. [More detail than has been included above!]

But I think the embarrassment is secondary to the fact that what Mr Black has been saying to us and what has been coming to us on Saturday nights is for all of us. I had had a terrible battle to get to my feet to actually come forward for ministry, and I would simply like to reinforce what he has read and to say that the thing that happened for me on the floor there last Sunday night has not gone away, and is terribly closely linked to what has been flowing in our midst. At a natural level I had thought that perhaps I wouldn't have to go forward for ministry. I had thought that if I just opened myself in my own quietness in my own home, Christ would come to me. And He had graciously come to me.

But there was something quite different in that ministry and in that going into the deep, deep atmosphere of Heaven. There was an awareness of Christ which totally excluded all awareness of self. And just as I think about it, it is not unrelated to what has already been in our midst. I remember coming home from our August camp, having caught a quality of stillness in the atmosphere which to me was tremendous power; it was tremendous inner stillness, and in it there was phenomenal power. And I just knew that if I could abide in that place then there would be power in my life, not just for myself but power for service. I have touched it on and off over the months intervening since the August camp. But I am more convinced tonight that the way into the glory and the way into the revival is the way of deep inner stillness, a deep inner death to ourself, that we might be rich and alive and rejoicing in our God.

Irene put her finger on something that was true of God's moving in our midst: although what happened from the end of 1994 was new, it was not totally different from all that had gone before. There had been a deep preparation for it. As Sarah said in her testimony (recorded in chapter 3), the Christ she met while prostrate on the floor was the Christ she already knew and loved. Irene's experience, though profoundly new in one sense, also reminded her of earlier experiences including her initial baptism in the Spirit.

There was nevertheless a quality about this new moving of God that was by its very nature 'other'. When God came to me at High Wycombe, I sensed Him, I sensed an atmosphere; I sensed an upper dimension. I felt I was in that dimension and have felt it around me ever since. It is with me morning, noon and night. I was aware of it when writing the new hymns, one of which in particular captures the innerness of that dimension. While writing it, I was living in that other world, feeling the things that are on paper:

Within the Veil

There's a road that is open before us
And it leads to a world unknown;
Oft have we pondered its pleasures
And pictured the heavenly throne.

We have thought of myriad angels,
Of harps and of jubilant song;
We have pictured our Lord and our Saviour
Where they praise Him all the day long.

But now our heavenly Guide
Is taking us upward from earth,
And we're entering spiritual hallways
With the sense of a spiritual birth.

There's a sensing of realms that we know not,
An acute awareness of need
To learn of the things of the Spirit,
To sit at God's table and feed.

The Lamb whom we pictured we see not
With the eyes of the flesh or our mind –
But we sense His ineffable nearness
As He opens the eyes of the blind.

Instruct us, our God and our Father,
As we move in this heavenly place;
Teach us the laws of the kingdom
As we bathe in Thy glory and grace.

Set our minds firmly on Jesus
As we search for that radiant face;
Let our feet go fervently forward
As we seek for that uttermost place –

Sing we now the song of Jesus,
Let the vaults of heaven ring;
Let all nations come and worship
At the throne of heaven's king.

Seek we now the joy of Jesus,
Seek the deepest wells of life;
Let us rise and take the kingdom,
Rise victorious in the strife.

We had had our intellectual conceptions, but the world
we were entering was largely unknown to all of us. But it
was happening as our eyes were being opened: it was not
just thought about. The throbbing of the very life of God
had come into the church.

A later book in the series describes the experiences of
others (such as Grace Gault and Diana Rutherford, both
used richly in ministering to others) who were already deep
in God and then found new depths in the uncharted ocean
of His beauty, holiness and power.

Notes

[1] From John Greenleaf Whittier's hymn 'Dear Lord and Father of mankind'.

[2] Compare Janet's testimony in chapter 2, and note 3 of the same chapter.

Chapter 8

To Fall or Not to Fall

'Should I go for ministry? Am I missing something by not going forward? I've listened to some of the testimonies from people who have been prostrate, and they have obviously met God in a major, some in a wonderful, way. If I don't go forward, may I be missing something that God has for me? . . . On the other hand, I haven't felt particularly like going forward, and how is a person to know? What ought I to do? I get my eye on what God has done for other people, and it's confusing me. I don't really know what I ought to do.'

There were, I thought, many people in a position of uncertainty. Some were very careful, and some were much more spiritually adventurous, taking the attitude, 'Well, I don't know either, but I'm going forward anyway. Nothing very harmful is likely to happen to me, and I'll experience this for myself.' Different attitudes were taken by different types of personality.

Some responses were more unusual than others.

This was true of **Pauline**,[1] who as one of my co-workers had witnessed many prostrations and revelled in the sense of blessing both for herself and others without the slightest sense that she should herself ask for ministry. What eventually brought her to change her mind was, she said, curiosity – though not, I think, of the idle variety.

The experience that has changed me happened in a house meeting in Darvel (Ayrshire) which over the months has been very significant for me. On some occasions God has come and something new has happened. On this occasion there were very few present. When we turned to prayer, I had no particular sense that God was going to do anything for me. But I suppose over recent days a natural curiosity had come in: I'll put it as bluntly as that. Indeed on one occasion after praying with someone I felt I couldn't continue standing on my own two feet. Though I had felt deep anointing while praying, it was when I went back to my seat that I realized my whole body was shaking so much that I couldn't stand up. Still, I did not go down.

I had heard many testimonies from people going forward for prayer, and had been there when many of them were prayed for, and it had been glorious. And I had thought, 'O God, You have been meeting all these people in these wonderful ways,' but I had never particularly felt any need or desire to go forward myself, because God was so much with me just as I was in the meetings. The blessing and glory of God coming down left me so full that I felt God had met all my need.

Now I can't say that on the occasion in Darvel I felt a tremendous sense of need. But in my spirit was the thought, 'Lord, if I went out tonight, would You meet me?' He didn't say yes or no: there was absolutely nothing like that.

I decided, 'Right. I'm going to experiment here!'

It sounds terribly cold and callous but actually wasn't. My attitude was, 'God, if You have something for me I want it. And if I go forward and nothing happens, I'm not going to be disappointed, because I haven't built myself up.'

I got up from my seat and said to Mr Black, 'I'm going to experiment.'

And an incredible experiment it turned out to be!

I had no preconceived ideas, none at all. But there was one thing in my mind: I was absolutely determined I wasn't going down unless the power of God came on me. As long as I could stand on my feet I was staying on my feet. Now there was no rebellion. But I just knew inside that if God was going to meet me He would have to put me down Himself. I would have to come to a stage where I couldn't stand.

I had asked someone to stand behind me, and actually said to them, 'Look, I might not go down – so don't worry! Be there, just in case.'

Pauline says that she will never forget what happened next.

The moment we turned to prayer, there was an immense power. Though it did not come like a bolt from heaven, it was nevertheless power such as I have never experienced in that quality in my life before. Now I remember the power that came with my baptism in the Spirit and totally transformed my life so that I was never the same again. A different type of power came upon me a year or two later when I received deliverance, and I was never the same after that. But last night it was completely different again. The only way I can describe it is this. It was as though inwardly I was falling, not backward as do many, but forward. As the power came down it was like falling and falling and falling into blackness.[2] It wasn't a terrifying blackness: nothing like that. But I actually thought I was going to pass out, and stopped just short of a complete loss of consciousness. I remember thinking, 'I can still stand' ... then it became totally impossible. I fell not backwards, but just like a sack of potatoes right down on the floor – literally crashing on my knees to the floor.

In that moment Pauline encountered a quality of God that she had never met at that depth before:

> In the blackness (I don't even like to call it that, but it was; it was a darkness) it wasn't the soft, gentle love of God that I met, but the absolute awe of God. There is no other word for it. Sometimes you hear people talk glibly about God and blame God for this and that. I thought, 'You can't! You cannot trifle with this God; you can't blame God for anything.' Scriptures have been living for me today that never lived all my Christian life – meaningful to a level, but never as they are now: scriptures like Isaiah 6:5 – *I am undone*. Just lying there at His feet I felt literally undone. There came the knowledge that even the smallest sin cannot stand before that awesome God.
>
> I had been on my knees with my head right down on the floor, but there came a point where I stretched out prostrate before God. For a considerable time I couldn't even speak in tongues; I could only say, 'O God – O God.' It was perhaps fifteen or twenty minutes later that I got up, dazed. I did not want to talk. I remember going upstairs for a minute and standing on the stairs on the way down, feeling I couldn't go back into company. When someone tried to talk, I could only nod a bit and say uh-huh; there were no words. It was so good to get home to an empty house, with no messages on the answering machine!

The next day Pauline walked outside in the quietness, taking in what God had done.

> What has interested me is that God knows what we need. I couldn't have told you that I needed that experience. But afterwards I felt, 'God, you knew what I needed. You knew that there was an area of

my being that needed a touch of the awesome reality of God.' I still feel it inside. It is as though I have been hit over the head and been absolutely dazed. I can still feel the sense of awe, a quietness inside. I can never be the same again – not that one wants to be the same again.

The strange thing is this. Over the years I have had a tremendous sense of the love and kindness of God which is beautiful, and I have always loved it. God has been exceedingly gentle with me. When I thought about the awe and the fear of God, my reaction was, 'Oh, but, God, I don't know if I want that revelation.' But in meeting this new aspect of His personality, there is a feeling, 'God, I want more of this.' The love and the gentleness, yes, I want that too. But there is something in this that I can hardly put into words, and that I don't understand at a mental level myself: something which I feel instinctively will open out into a vast, vast expanse where the deep burning fire of God will burn steadily and purely with tremendous power. I feel that it is a realm of fire, a realm of cleanness, of holiness and awe.

Pauline referred to the darkness. My attention was first drawn to this by James Salter of the Congo (now Zaire) Evangelistic Mission, whose grave was dug when he nearly died in central Africa. He felt himself wonderfully enfolded by a black velvet curtain as he was sinking into eternity – though God brought him back to life. There is a blackness that is the blackness of hell; but there is that lovely darkness of which several have spoken, which is the gateway to God: you go through that.

It is intriguing that Pauline's twin sister **Susie** showed a somewhat similar independence of mind.[3] In Susie's case, the attitude was one of: 'I'm not going for ministry just because everyone else is going for ministry!' Like Pauline, she was thoroughly supportive of the new ministry, and was finding God richly in the meetings where she sat or assisted in 'catching' others. But her route into her own time of ministry and its outcome was rather different.

As I saw people testify week after week to the moving of God in their lives, I thrilled with the wonder of it in every part of my being. The first time it happened in High Wycombe it left a profound sense of God on my life. I was impressed by the utter control of God coming down on the life of an individual receiving ministry. As a result I was always very open, thinking, 'O God, if ever You say the word, I'll be right out there.'

But oddly enough I never really felt God say, 'Right, Susie, tonight's the night for you!'

Yet I found that over the weeks God met me remarkably just where I sat. I kept a diary of what was happening, and encouraged others in our house meeting to do the same – for we can so quickly forget even wonderful things that God does.

One Sunday morning early in 1995 Mary was ministering and she asked me if I would catch some-one. Now I absolutely hate catching people; I just can't do it. I landed on the deck with somebody once! Eventually I said to my husband Paul, 'Show me how to catch people: what do you do?' – because he always seems to be able to catch them without hurting himself or landing with them! And I said, 'Right, I'll try and catch you!'

And then I said, 'No, no! don't fall back any more!'

But I was very obedient and followed Mary across the hall. As she prayed with this person I became intensely aware of the anointing and the power of God on Mary and flowing out through her into the other person. Overwhelmed with wonder, I duly caught them as best I was able. Turning to walk away, I found that I was actually staggering myself with the overflow of what had been coming into that life. And it's funny the things that go through your mind. I remember looking across to where I was supposed to be going, and thinking, 'There are two bodies I've got to step over to get there. I'm just not going to be able to do it.' I just made it, grabbing hold of a ledge to steady myself en route.

This experience had a profound effect on me. There were also a couple of other incidents, one of which happened later that morning, when by a miracle something was absolutely changed for a lifetime: something that had probably been there for about three years was gone in a moment of time.

These were wonderful experiences, but to Susie's mind they by no means constituted a reason for going out for ministry herself. When she went to the Greenock prayer meeting one Monday night, it was simply to be where God was and to be open to whatever He was doing – where she sat.

But I thought otherwise! As Susie put it:

Then Mr Black hauled me up!

Now the one thing I always felt was that I did not want to go for ministry just because everybody else was going for it. As the weeks passed, I would look around and think, 'Well, more or less everybody else has gone! Who is there left?' (I did find there was one person who hadn't gone, who was having a good look at me that Monday night!)

I thought, 'God, if You want to do something I am a hundred per cent open. I am so thankful for what You have done just where I sat, and for the true, life-changing testimonies to what You have done in other people's lives. But no way can I go out just because everybody else in the church has gone out.'

But Mr Black pulled me out!

I said, 'Look, I'm not getting prayed with just because everybody else is being prayed with. I'm not!' So we were having this little discussion while the prayer time was going on.

I said, 'I am completely open; I have stood in spirit right behind you from the moment that this started. I've been a hundred per cent with you!' I really had spiritually supported everything that had happened. But I was adamant that I was not going to be prayed with merely because every single other person in the church had been prayed with (even if it had been true).

'OK,' I said, 'you can pray with me, but don't be disappointed if nothing happens!' It's dreadful, isn't it?

So we turned to prayer, and the same lovely sense of God that had been present in the prayer meeting as people had been ministered to was very much there. But I can't honestly say that I felt, 'Right, Susie, God's wanting to put you down,' although I was very open and relaxed. After a few minutes, Mary came up as well and as we prayed a lovely feeling came over me like that of falling asleep at the point where you can still fight it but you feel it would be much easier just to drift off. After a particularly busy day, to feel so relaxed was a most agreeable sensation.

I found myself staggering and feeling it would be so easy just to give in to this, just to slip into it ... And that is exactly what I did.

Susie's next comment is a revealing one. There were many, I think, to whom it could have applied. Indeed, is there any man or woman alive to whom it might not apply?

Many of us, I think, have at least a subconscious feeling that when we are going to meet with God we are going to get a severe scolding. But it wasn't like that at all. It was very quiet, it was very undramatic, but it was beautiful. It was just that God was there.

There was a sense of His peace and of His loveliness. And one part of you wants to say, 'But, God, it's me, it's **me** that You're talking to, it's me that You're actually pouring this out on!' You feel so unworthy. But in thinking of your unworthiness you are thinking of yourself, and I felt in that moment that God did not want me to think about myself, my own unworthiness – me, me, me – but just to go out into Christ and accept the loveliness, the love and the peace that He was pouring down.

I could have stayed there all night. Afterwards I sat on the floor for a long time in silence, just being with God in that place of utter quietness, utter peace. In that spiritual realm there is almost a silence of eternity, and yet in it there is vibrant life. It is 'where we live and move and have our being in God,' where there is the loveliness of Christ, the absolute loveliness of our God.

Susie's verdict was that her experience had been well worth waiting for! With unconscious humour, she announced in effect that she was subsequently not only open to whatever else God might have for her, but in a position to encourage any other isolated malingerer to come! As she earnestly put it:

You are meeting with a God who loves you, you are meeting with a God who cares, you are meeting with a God who knows you far better than you know yourself.

There can be an amusing side even to deeply spiritual events. One wonders if there is sometimes a smile on the face of the Divine Angler as He plays His fish and watches its stratagems for avoiding the blessing He is about to impart. The question of 'going down' deeply exercised the minds of many people. It was, after all, the point at which control over one's physical being was voluntarily surrendered to the Spirit. But **Anita**'s concern about falling was more altruistic than most. A qualified nurse and nursery worker, Anita describes how God met her:

One Saturday night sitting through the meeting I felt that God was speaking to me on a certain issue and telling me that He wanted to take it. It was as if He placed a burden on me that would make me go forward to have it lifted.

While this was happening, I was reflecting, 'I just know that I can't go forward like that.' All that I could think about was the poor person that was going to be catching me!

I thought, 'It's all very well for other people to go forward – they're quite light, and people can catch them quite easily. But if I go forward and somebody comes to pray with me and I fall back, then I'm likely going to flatten the person who's trying to catch me!'

Deep down, I didn't want to fall on top of anybody and hurt them. I thought God might meet me in some other way. But as time went on I knew that I had to get up and go forward. Mr Black took me on to the platform and told me where to stand. My mind was rattling with these thoughts, and I decided I would say to whoever came to pray with me, 'Is it all right if I sit or kneel down?' or something like that. But when I got up on to the platform I thought, 'What's the point in worrying about it? Just forget about it until the time comes.' While Mr Black was walking down to space other people out along the aisles, I closed my eyes and started going through to God myself. I just said, 'Jesus.'

Without anyone near me, all of a sudden I saw a light. My eyes were closed; but it was like a physical light coming towards me and on to my face. It pushed me back, and I fell down on to the floor. I didn't even think about that – I was so preoccupied with the thought that someone would lay hands on me. And

God did it in a different way! It's as if He saw how I was feeling! While lying on the carpet, I felt Him putting a blanket of peace over me, from my head right down to my toes. Lying there and resting in Christ, I felt Him breathing life into me and cleansing me. It was as if He breathed into my mouth and the breath was going down into my lungs, filling me up and pouring back out in a cleansing process. I felt totally secure in Christ.

It wasn't till I began to get back up that I felt pain all down the right side of my neck; I mentioned it to one or two people. (I remembered hitting my head off something when I had fallen back.) In spite of the pain, Christ was really close to me. Feeling His presence so much with me, it didn't really bother me that I had the pain at all.

Back home as I lay in bed, I was still in that presence of Christ. Opening my Bible I read the New Year word [4] over again, and a thought went through my mind: 'I wonder how I'm going to get to sleep tonight, because my neck's quite sore?' It was just a passing thought – and the minute I thought it, I felt the pain going right out of my neck. I could hardly believe it: I began moving my neck and there was just no pain there at all. Christ had taken it away from me.

I have felt a change throughout the week. I have been walking much closer to Christ and feeling His presence with me much more deeply in various ways. Especially when praying there is deeper communion with Christ than I have ever had, just sensing Him. I was out delivering leaflets for the nursery up in Glasgow recently, and a point came when I was really fed up and tired. Then I turned my mind to Christ and felt Him coming near and walking with me, and I don't know if I've felt that so much for years, really ... maybe when I first became a Christian: just that presence of Christ continually with me and walking with me in communion. I praise His Name for what He has done.

Anita's testimony was closely followed by that of **Alison**,[5] who commented humorously that

it never crossed my mind who was going to catch me! I think I assumed with an innocent faith that I would go down like a feather – and you'll have to ask whether that was true or not: I couldn't tell you!

Alison went on to describe her initial reaction to the new ministry against the background of her expectations for the year 1994:

Last year, away back at the New Year time, we were promised that it would be a year of the revelation of the glory of God. I, in common with many people here, found that the glory that came upon us in that year was something new and deep and rich and full. About the beginning of November I told Mary one night how I felt God had spoken to me and said, 'Don't let this year gutter out. Don't just say, "Well, that's November. That's that year passing," but I was actually to look for a deeper incoming of that glory as the year drew to a close. I set myself firmly, determined not to slacken, but really to look for an incoming of that glory, and I felt I knew what it would be like. It would be more of that beautiful presence that comes to us so often on a Saturday night, and it would be deeper and richer.

It was a terrible shock to me when shortly afterwards Mr Black came back from his meeting with God in High Wycombe with all his news of a new ministry and a new wave. I was completely thrown by it. To tell you the truth, it wasn't what I wanted. I wanted more of the glory that we knew, and I wanted to be exactly sure of the ground on which I stood.

And every change is a crisis, isn't it? It was certainly a crisis for me. I found in the week succeeding his return that all sorts of thoughts were going through my mind: 'What is this? Why are we changing? What we had was wonderful. Can I tune to this?' But just as the week drew to a close I started to recognize that really there was an awful lot of assault in the matter. The deep incoming of God was being challenged, I think in many people, with thoughts that we couldn't understand and the fear of a place that we weren't secure in.

I made up my mind right at the beginning just to lay that all to rest and to go out for ministry and to look for God to come. I hadn't a specific burden. Anita said she knew God was speaking to her. In my own case there wasn't anything that I was aware of; I just felt that this was the way God was leading us, and it was right to be supportive of that ministry and receiving from God the blessing that He undoubtedly had for us.

Having settled the matter thus, Alison duly went forward at the next opportunity:

As I fell to the floor, I was aware of Mr Black saying a strange thing – because it was the last thing on my mind. He said, 'Here, Lord, is one of your servants who has suffered much.' Though it was the last thought in my mind I just let it come, and I lay at peace. Suddenly I felt a tear running out of one eye down the side of my face and right through my hair ... Eventually I got up and went back to my seat.

Alison did not yet fully understand all that God had done in her. It was not until a few weeks later at the next New Year conference, during a time of waiting before God, that she discovered the deep change that had taken place:

Mrs Gault came to pray with me, as she has done faithfully over many a conference. Often when she comes to pray there is a particular anointing of God that comes through her to me, and it always does the same thing. Now this isn't all that ever happens to me when Grace prays with me; sometimes it can be totally different and very glorious. But I know this particular anointing. When it comes on me there is a feeling as if deep, deep inside there is a place that is terribly hurt, almost like a scarred part of my being. And somehow when she comes it's as if the anointing that's there takes a plaster off that hurt – and anybody who's ever taken a plaster off a hurt knows it's agony. When she has come and that anointing has come and I have felt that place touched, tears have come copiously. I've cried and cried and felt the agony of it, and (to be honest) as soon as she's gone away I've very quickly slapped a plaster back on that sore place. I've thought, 'I don't want to think about that. Life must go on. Everybody's got sufferings in their life; everyone's had trials and difficulties. No point in dwelling on things like that. Just get up and get on with life.' And I've put it away and firmly refused to think about it.

This time again I felt that anointing come with her. I prepared to experience the pain again, knowing that it was changing and getting less as the years passed, but expecting another episode of that same sort of thing. She came, and I felt God come deeply, deeply inside me. A feeling of rejoicing came from within – a happiness, a sense of wholeness, of completeness, of oneness. I realized to my amazement that all of that pain was gone – just utterly gone. I found myself looking for it in the place where it had been – like the girl Mr Black prayed for who started looking for her vanished lump, or like Mr Black himself who tells us how he looked for the pain in his hip when it was healed. I was looking for this hurt; it was as real as a physical pain in the inner being: and it was utterly, utterly gone. As I rejoiced in God, the knowledge came to me that that was the work that He had done for me that earlier night. When I had been there on His operating table, He had taken from me a burden of pain that I had carried for many, many years.

Alison realized that her experience could be helpful for others:

> I would like to encourage those who may think, 'I don't know what I need.' God knows what you need. As for those who do not yet see exactly what has happened to you, I think that as time goes by you will find yourself in circumstances where you realize, 'I've changed. That's different. That's gone.' It is a wonderful opportunity that has come to the church, that we have a ministry not dictated by ourselves ('God, I want this'), not dictated by other people, but dictated by God Himself. He knows what we need and is able to free us from all grief, from all pain, and from all sin. Blessed be His Name.

Notes

[1] Pauline Anderson (see chapter 1, note 5).

[2] Grace Gault records a similar experience in the second book of this trilogy.

[3] Susie Sharkey (née Anderson) tells the story of her conversion and early years in Christ in my book *The Incomparable Christ*.

[4] See chapter 2, note 3.

[5] Alison Speirs (see chapter 5, note 2).

Chapter 9

A Rich Foreshadowing

Every year for the last thirty years or more God has given a prophetic word to the Struthers group of churches at New Year time. It is enshrined in a verse or verses of Scripture which had particular application to the incoming year. These verses are referred to as 'the New Year Word'. When the new moving of God began in November 1994 there were those who noticed how it dovetailed with the word that had been given at the start of the year. Some of our number spoke publicly of it.

One was **Jennifer Jack**, the leader of our Falkirk church. She noted:

> God is bringing into being something new in the realm of ministry. Large numbers of people have found their needs met very particularly and in a kind of mass way, rather than with individual counselling and individual ministry.
>
> This to my mind has been tied up very much with the sense of a promise given twelve months ago about the glory of God coming down into the midst of us. Remember when Solomon dedicated the temple the priests couldn't stand to minister because of the glory of God. I think an aspect of that has actually become apparent in the ministry: there is the sense that we are coming nearer the place where God works

directly with people almost without human channel at all. It is the kind of thing that happens again and again in revival, when there comes such an awesome weight of His presence and His glory that those who have been ministering may stand aside because the Holy Spirit is working so directly. I don't mean that there are not times for individual ministry. But there is the sense of the drawing near of His glory in a way akin to what we read of in revival. I feel that in this year we have stepped much closer to the outworking of what God intends in these last days.

Another who believed God had shown something of what lay ahead was **Diana Rutherford**, leader of our Cumbernauld work:

Around the middle of December 1993 I felt the Holy Spirit ask me to do something that He had never asked me to do before in quite that way. He seemed to ask me to go out in my spirit into the future for the coming year and to find out what the Spirit had for us as a (local) church.

As I went out I realized that I was losing consciousness of the people in the meeting which I was taking. Unsure whether this was right, I opened myself and felt the Spirit tell me to go out further. In doing so, I actually lost consciousness of being in a meeting with others around me and was caught up in the Spirit. I saw an angelic being standing in the heavens, and to its left I saw an open door of fire: the edges of it were made of fire, and through that doorway was fire, pure fire. Without words, without hearing a voice, but knowing the communication that comes in heavenly places, I heard the angel speak to me or transmit thought to me: 'This year (1994) will be a year of the revelation of the glory of God to the church.' And he bid me come up higher. As I went I came close to the door and saw through the doorway the glory of God, the God Jehovah. I was afraid to go through the door; I found my flesh pull back, wanting to come out of the Spirit. Part of me wanted to draw back, but another part wanted to go in.

As I waited, I knew instinctively that to go through that doorway would cost me far more than anything I had ever been asked to pay before. My immediate reaction was: 'Lord, I don't know how it can cost any more. I feel as though I have given everything. I don't understand how it can cost any more. But I want to go on and I want to go in.' Just for a minute I felt my spirit cross that line, as it were, and go into the glory, but only for a minute. And I knew that the coming year would fulfil that word to my own life.

It was about ten days later that Diana came to the New Year conference in 1994 to hear Mary Black say, 'This year is to be a year of the revelation of the glory of God.'

I could have fallen off my seat, and yet in some ways I wasn't surprised. Some time after that I came across this reading that summed up perfectly my experience:

> *After this I looked, and there before me was a door standing open in heaven. And the voice I had first heard speaking to me like a trumpet said, 'Come up here, and I will show you what must take place after this.' At once I was in the Spirit, and there before me was a throne in heaven with someone sitting on it. And the one who sat there had the appearance of jasper.* (Revelation 4:1–3)

It was so perfect: *the voice I had first heard speaking to me* was *like a trumpet*. It said, *Come up here*, and when I did so *I looked, and there before me was a door standing open in heaven*. It was exactly as I had seen it.

And through the year God has fulfilled His word to me in my heart. It has cost. But there is nothing to be compared with the glory that shall be revealed to us, and I have found this year to be a year of tremendous revelation. I feel as though I have come to know God the Father, God Almighty, in a way I have never known Him before. I have had more revelation of eternity than I have ever had before.

During that year, Diana said, she found a door almost continuously open.

I remember the point in the year when I felt as though I crossed through that doorway and went into an almost permanent condition of abiding in a new depth of the glory of God such as I had never known. It was towards the end of this year that the new ministry was born in the church, and somehow I felt so much part of that. It began at the London (High Wycombe) conference, but it was not until the ministry actually came into being in Greenock that I went home with a knowledge that the cloud of the glory of God had come upon the movement. I went back to Cumbernauld and to my delight discovered that that same cloud of glory was in our Sunday services. On the third Sunday night as I was ministering to different individuals I found that they began to go down one after the other: and none of them knew that anyone else had gone down. There was a sense that the cloud of the glory had come and, independently of each other, people were going down under the power of the Spirit. It was lovely to know that it had come.

On the relation between the new ministry and other older ones Diana had this to say:

Being open to the Holy Spirit since then, I have discovered that the new ministry does not replace any ministry that is already in the church. There is not a sense in which anybody that I now pray with must go down under the power of the Spirit. The anointing is sometimes the kind I am more used to. But I find at different times that the new anointing has come very, very strongly. I remember once in our Wednesday night Bible study, I wasn't expecting the move of the Holy Spirit in that way. We had been having a prayer time during which I had been ministering. The Holy Spirit had been there in the way that we are so used to, and ministry had been very good. I actually sat down with the intention of closing the meeting, but just as I did so the power came, that presence came, that cloud of the glory of God came, and one person after another began to go down, some without any ministry at all. God was there.

The effect on one life was related by Diana in chapter 2 of this book; elsewhere she describes how others found their way into the riches of God.[1]

Finally, my daughter **Mary Black**, through whom the 1994 Word had been given, had this to say when reviewing the year:

As the word came that 1994 would be a year of the revelation of His glory, I became aware of an awesomeness of power: an awesomeness of the glory of God towards which He was pointing.

When my father came back from the conference when he was first used in the ministry that had come into being, I remember him telling me in our own living room of what had happened. As soon as he started speaking, there was a witness in my spirit: 'This is holy. This is the real thing.' I could feel the light round about him; I could feel the mantle on him; I could feel the room fill up with light.

The Awe of God

I have often looked at that passage about Ananias and Sapphira, and wondered at the quality of the presence of God in which telling a lie brought about their death. Somehow just for a moment I glimpsed that quality, that measure of power, and the awesomeness of God. You do not trifle with this, you do not tamper with this, you do not have any kind of duplicity, or shiftiness, or lying: you have nothing but stark truth in the presence of this God.

As we came up to the Saturday night on which Mr Black was first used in that ministry in Greenock, I was standing on the platform, and it was like standing in a bath of light. I am quite sure that many, like myself, felt an awesome grip of God and took a step backwards. A fear of the living God came upon many of us that night. And there came revelation of the church putting up barriers through which God could not come until we lifted them from the inside. I think we glimpsed a measure of that which has to come (as my father has spoken about at times) – a quality of conviction of sin and of thundering power that shall sweep the land. And there was a measure of fear: fear of God coming this close, fear of God entering in so deeply to our individual lives.

I was deeply moved by Mary's words. When I had told her what had happened at High Wycombe I had not been quite sure how she would react. She had not said very much at the time. Now my spiritual life is not dependent on the reaction of anybody in the whole wide world. It has never been that way. But I knew these hours in High Wycombe and the hours that immediately followed had been amongst the happiest I had ever lived through in a long lifetime. I knew and sensed the presence of God. When speaking to Mary, I had not known she was seeing light, or what she felt in the room. But I knew God. When that first hymn, 'The Song of Jesus', came to me, my spirit was in a degree of ecstasy, out in another world – and so with the other hymns that came. When Mary spoke of that power that she sensed where Ananias and Sapphira were concerned, I could understand her. We had come to a holy place, a holy anointing, the holy God.

Speaking to the assembled church at the turn of the year Mary commented on the mixed reactions of the people:

> In varying degrees we have responded. We have either laid aside the fear and gone as far as we can in God, or perhaps we have tried to adjust to externals and even been prepared if so directed by God to go forward and go down. But, you know, going forward and going prostrate doesn't necessarily mean that you are actually yielding everything or lifting all the barriers against God from your life. In varying degrees we have responded to the action of the Divine, but there is an element of awe mingled with fear and with the knowledge that this is a God not to be trifled with. This is a God who knows our sin, a God who expects action and change and deep fundamental adjustment of inner being and of lifestyle to His commandment and to His claims. There are so many ways in which we dodge round this fundamental issue, that God wants change. We are not satisfying Him by being prepared to have a solitary dramatic experience lying on the floor. That is not satisfying His requirements. It may be a part of His way into His purpose for our lives. But we know deep inside that it is change and adjustment that are demanded by God.

Mary went on to say that she felt that God was offering a season of mercy:

> I felt He was saying to me that He would give us a season of grace in which He would lift or withhold in a measure the terribleness of His power to give us time for adjustment. He would pour out copiously and marvellously of His grace, mercy and love. He showed me the land of promise that He has stretched

before us, and the desire of His heart for us to enter into a place of wealth and abundance in the things of His Spirit. He showed me His desire for us to come into the place of His appointment and of His provision – a land that is wide and wealthy and without horizons. And He showed me some of the qualities that lie within that land.

The angel said when Jesus was born, *Fear not* (Luke 2:10 AV). And indeed every time there was an angelic encounter the recipient was afraid. To the shepherds the words were, *Peace to men on whom his favour rests* (Luke 2:14). And I feel that God would give this reassurance, this overwhelming reassurance that in that land there is peace, safety and well-being; there is security in that land and the provision of the fullness of God, a wide, wide wealth.

Principally and overwhelmingly, what He showed me was His love ... His love ... His love. The other side of the awe of God is His love. The other side of that terrible, awesome power that makes us know that we are but dust, shrivelled into nothing in His sight were He to release it unmercifully – the other side of that is an unimaginable wealth and abundance of love. In that land into which He would take us I can see the flowing streams, the trees that are rich with fruit, the rivers irrigating the soil. What folly of the human heart to stay outside such a land in poverty, penury and want, to stay circumscribed by the self-life, to allow fear to hold us back – our fear of what God will take from us, and what He will ask of us, and what depth of change will be wrought in our lives!

Do you know, it is the devil who tells us, 'Don't go in there: you'll have nothing for yourself. You'll not be able to handle it. It's too large a dimension; it's scary, it's terrifying.' In that very first moment when the awesomeness of God draws near, your spirit is attracted, and it is the flesh and the devil that rear up in a resistance to the breakthrough of the power of the almighty God. A picture is given to you that makes you scared – humanly, naturally scared – to go right into the land of promise. And God would give a season when there is sea upon sea of the mercy and the grace of the Lord Jesus Christ.

Read of the Welsh revival: how glorious! Oh, yes, there was conviction of sin. But oh, the joy of release from sin! Oh, the celebration of the Lamb of God, and of the power of the blood of Jesus which comes into the hearts of men and women throughout the church of Jesus Christ! Oh, the seasons of ecstasy and of bliss, of praising and of singing! What a wealth of wonderful hymns have poured out, cascaded through the ages, from seasons of revival! Are they hymns of fear and pain and agony? No! They are hymns of joy, of glory, of livingness, of love. For the God who created us is the God who has loved us from everlasting to everlasting.

When Mary predicted a time of the extended grace and love of God to let people come quietly into the deeps of His presence, I was reminded of the warning that my late co-leader Miss Taylor used to give: 'Come while you can before you are driven. Let your sin be cleared away privately with God, because if you are caught in the day of God's power it will come tumbling forth publicly: you will not be able to retain it.'[2] Such is the hour of the power of God.

As Mary spoke, I thought ahead. A time of grace, a time of beauty, a time of the gentleness of Christ: I rejoiced in that. But my spirit began to be ambitious, and I wondered. When would be the hour of the floods of God, when the high tides rise: the day of the power of God, the iron of God that breaks the nations, the day of the drive of the Divine, when men and women break before Him and great power floods the land: the day that comes after the gentleness? I pondered as I realized that through almost all of a lifetime that has been my own ultimate ambition: to see that day when His power is unleashed: the great power of the great God.

Then I thought, 'I'll have a dilemma, as Kathryn Kuhlman once did.' At one time she wanted Christ to take her home but then became so thrilled with what God was doing that she did not want to go before His time. I can see a dilemma between saying, 'Lord, spare me while I see the full floods flow,' and, 'Lord, I have seen Thy power. Now let Thy servant depart in peace.'

> *Prayer*: Lord, show us the day of Your power. Lord, we have stood through long years. We have seen Jerusalem trodden down, seen wickedness coming in as a flood, seen the derision poured upon Your people, heard the laughter of Satan, and, Lord, we don't like it. There rises a fighting spirit that will not have it, Lord. It shall not forever be that way. The Lion of the tribe of Judah shall triumph, and He'll tread down His enemies, and He'll crush them underfoot, and the day of gentleness shall pass to the day of iron, and the glory of the Lord shall come. Oh, blessed be the Name of the Lord, the tide shall turn and wickedness shall be driven before the blast of God. Lord, put the fight of God in our spirit. Take us through the days of the gentleness and the love of Christ, but make us ready to draw the sword, and, Lord, not just to be left with the hilt of a sword in our hand, but with the sharp sword of the word of God, riding in triumph following the Lion, following the train of the Son of God, quelling the nations by Your great power. Lord, be with Your people, we pray You, in Christ's Name and for His sake. Amen.

Notes

[1] For further events in Cumbernauld, including Diana's own meeting with God, see the second book of this trilogy.

[2] Miss Elizabeth H. Taylor was a founder member and co-leader of our movement until her death in 1991. Her story is told in part 2 of my book *A Trumpet Call to Women* (New Dawn Books, 1988). More about her spiritual life and ministry can be found in a more recent book compiled by myself and entitled *E.H. Taylor, A Modern Christian Mystic: Sayings and Recollections* (New Dawn Books, 1994).

Note to Readers

If you would like to enquire further about issues raised in this book or if you feel that the compiler could be of help, you are invited to write to him at 27 Denholm Street, Greenock, PA16 8RH, Scotland, or telephone 01475-729668 or 01475-787432.

It may also be of interest to know that Hugh Black is normally involved in five conferences in Scotland each year – New Year, Easter, July, August and October. Friends gather from many parts of Britain. An open invitation is extended to all and particularly to those interested in the baptism in the Holy Spirit and related themes. Details will be provided on enquiry.

Other Books by Hugh Black

The Baptism in the Spirit and Its Effects £4.99

Used in bringing people into the baptism in the Spirit and described as one of the clearest, most incisive books on the subject. This expanded edition includes evidence that Finney, Moody and Spurgeon spoke in tongues, and narrates miraculous effects of the baptism in the lives of Jimmy Lunan and Allan Wiggins.

Reflections on the Gifts of the Spirit £2.75

Deals in an original way with its subject. The chapters on miracles, healings and discernment (with exorcism) have roused great interest and led to positive action. Anecdotes and illustrations have been much appreciated.

Reflections on a Song of Love £1.25

A highly original commentary on 1 Corinthians 13. The drawing power of love pervades this fascinating study. The author shows very clearly how this chapter fully supports and in no way detracts from the doctrine of Pentecost.

A Trumpet Call to Women £2.50

Presents a strong case from Scripture for greater involvement of women in ministry. It throws much light on those portions which on the surface seem to put women in a subject role. It includes the testimony of Elizabeth H. Taylor, a lady much used of God. A stirring book, demanding a response – a call to action.

Consider Him £2.25

Considers a number of the qualities of Christ. He Himself seems to speak from the pages of the book, both in the main text and in the testimony of Jennifer Jack, whose selfless presentation truly leaves the reader to consider Christ.

Battle for the Body £2.95

It will take courage to face the truths highlighted in this original approach to fundamental issues of sanctification. The second part presents the powerful testimony of John Hamilton – a preacher widely known and loved.

The Clash of Tongues: With Glimpses of Revival £2.75

Part One is a commentary on 1 Corinthians 14. It deals in detail with some of the more difficult questions. Part Two deals with the relationship between revival and Pentecost and refers to the 1939 and 1949 revivals in Lewis, introducing a number of people who were involved in the first of these – particularly Mary MacLean, whose remarkable testimony is related. This book may particularly appeal to people studiously inclined.

The Incomparable Christ £2.75

Part One deals with the gospel. It faces honestly the questions of Christ's resurrection and that of all men.

It deals in a direct way with the doctrine of hell and eternal judgment, and gives practical instruction on the way of salvation. Part Two presents the remarkable testimonies of two young ladies.

Gospel Vignettes £2.95

Focuses attention on various facets of the gospel, with chapter titles like: Ye Must Be Born Again, The Life-Giving Water, Weighed in the Balances, Behold I Stand at the Door and Knock, The Hour of Decision. Includes testimonies of three people whose lives have been transformed by Christ, to one of whom Christ Himself appeared. Useful in the gospel, but introducing the Pentecostal dimension.

Reflections from Abraham £2.50

Outlines spiritual principles seen in the life of Abraham. It deals with his call and ours, the mountain as distinct from the valley life, intercession, Lot in Sodom, the sacrifice of Isaac and the way of faith. Part Two tells of the action of God in the life of Dorothy Jennings, to whom Abraham has been of particular significance.

Reflections from Moses:
With the Testimony of Dan McVicar £2.99

Part One shows the outworking of spiritual principles such as the calling and training of a man of God, the need to start from holy ground, deliverance from bondage, and the consequences of Moses' failure in a critical hour. Part Two presents the well-known evangelist Dan McVicar's story in his own words. The conversion of this militant communist and the intervention of God in the lives of his parents make thrilling reading.

Christ the Deliverer £2.99

Deals with both physical and spiritual deliverance. It includes a number of remarkable testimonies to healing, e.g. from blindness, manic depression, ME, rheumatoid arthritis, spinal injury, phobias, nightmares. It speaks of the appearance of angels, touches on revival and analyses the theory of 'visualization'.

Christian Fundamentals £3.50

Part One deals with the individual and his needs in the realms of Salvation, Baptism in the Spirit, and Deliverance. Part Two focuses on the outflow of the life of God to meet the needs of others through Vocal, Hidden and Open Power Ministries. The End Times are the subject of Part Three.

Reflections from David £3.75

This searching book shows a man after God's own heart in the glory of his achievements and the tragedy of his failings. Divine retribution and forgiveness, the joy of deliverance, and the action of God in present-day lives are all examined.

Pioneers of the Spiritual Way £4.99

From a lost Eden our race walked a lost road, occasionally experiencing higher things as pioneers of the spiritual way led upwards. The impassable barrier between God and man was finally removed as the last Adam blasted a way through: Christ, bringing many sons to glory.

Revival:
Including the Prophetic Vision of Jean Darnall £3.99

Some of the great revivals of the past are reviewed with their enduring principles and changing patterns. Revival comes nearer as we are confronted with more recent movements of God. The celebrated vision of

Jean Darnall has left many with a feeling of keen expectation for coming days.

Revival: Personal Encounters   £4.50

From the treasure chest of memory the author brings a series of revival-related incidents. We hear of Studd, Burton and Salter and of revival in the Congo and Rwanda. More is revealed of the moving of God in Lewis and at an unusual Scottish school camp. A contemporary scene in Brazil brings revival very close. The highly original testimony of Alison Speirs brings the fact and challenge right to our doorstep.

Revival: Living in the Realities   £3.99

For a revived or a revival-conscious people a high level of Christian living is immediately presented. The experience of revival has to be outworked. This book ponders issues such as spiritual warfare, what it means to be imitators of Christ, the need to progress from forgiveness to love for those who do us harm, and the mystery of the love of God itself. An unusual and thought-provoking approach.

E.H. Taylor: A Modern Christian Mystic:
Sayings and Recollections   £4.50

A sequel to *Trumpet Call to Women*, this highly unusual book contains insights into a wide range of spiritual themes on the part of one who was much used in predictive prophecy and in leading people into the baptism in the Spirit and deliverance, and especially into a deep knowledge of Christ.

War in Heaven and Earth   £6.99

This book illuminates the subject of spiritual warfare both at the 'ground level' of day-to-day living where the devil's weapons are met with the weapons of Christ, and at the unseen level of conflict where the power of Christ breaks the hold of spiritual entities over specific territorial areas.

Book Orders

New Dawn Bookshop, 10A Jamaica Street, Greenock
Renfrewshire, PA15 1YB, Scotland
Telephone 01475 729668   Fax 01475 728145

ORDER FORM

Please send me books by Hugh B. Black indicated below:

Quantity	Title	Price
_____	The Baptism in the Spirit and Its Effects	£4.99
_____	Reflections on the Gifts of the Spirit	£2.75
_____	Reflections on a Song of Love (A commentary on 1 Corinthians 13)	£1.25
_____	A Trumpet Call to Women	£2.50
_____	Consider Him (Twelve Qualities of Christ)	£2.25
_____	Battle for the Body	£2.95
_____	The Clash of Tongues: With Glimpses of Revival	£2.75
_____	The Incomparable Christ	£2.75
_____	Gospel Vignettes	£2.95
_____	Reflections from Abraham	£2.50
_____	Reflections from Moses: With the Testimony of Dan McVicar	£2.99
_____	Christ the Deliverer	£2.99
_____	Christian Fundamentals	£3.50

(cont. overleaf)

_____	Reflections from David	£3.75
_____	Pioneers of the Spiritual Way	£4.99
_____	Revival: Including the Prophetic Vision of Jean Darnall	£3.99
_____	Revival: Personal Encounters	£4.50
_____	Revival: Living in the Realities	£3.99
_____	E.H. Taylor: A Modern Christian Mystic	£4.50
_____	War in Heaven and Earth	£6.99
_____	A View from the Floor	£5.99

Name . . . .

Address . . . .

. . . .

. . . . Post Code . . . .

Please add 50p per book for postage and packing.